A Nation of Immigrants

"This is a gem of a short book written by a renowned scholar of biblical ethics but readable by all Christians. The experience and teaching of Israel, God's people who lived as sojourners and immigrants for most of their long history, is most appropriate for us today."

—CHARLES E. CURRAN
Perkins School of Theology, Southern Methodist University

"This lucid eighty-four-page book effectively retells the biblical story of God's people as aliens, refugees, and deportees who were greeted with xenophobia, persecution, and violence where they journeyed. Responding to this experience, they adopted laws providing equal protection and social welfare for aliens in Israelite lands. Emphasizing the biblical record of the intermarriage and kinship of all nations, Hiers thoughtfully reflects on how this story informs modern-day debates over immigration policy."

—MARIE FAILINGER
Mitchell Hamline School of Law

"This is a marvelous book—clear, concise, and penetrating. Hiers demonstrates that the Bible's sojourner was not some 'other' but was core both to the construction of Israel and to Israel's protection of sojourners."

—JONATHAN R. COHEN
University of Florida

"Marshalling years of serious study, Hiers condenses centuries of civilization into a coherent bundle of positive impressions from ages past. Then and now, strangers are not so strange after all. All are strangers facing strange circumstances . . . As Hiers rightly concludes, the legacy of biblical life and law is to diminish the stigma of foreignness."

—JOHN W. WELCH
Brigham Young University

A Nation of Immigrants

Sojourners in Biblical Israel's Tradition and Law

Richard H. Hiers

Foreword by David P. Gushee

RESOURCE *Publications* · Eugene, Oregon

A NATION OF IMMIGRANTS
Sojourners in Biblical Israel's Tradition and Law

Resource Publications
An Imprint of Wipf and Stock Publishers
199 W. 8th Ave., Suite 3
Eugene, OR 97401

www.wipfandstock.com

PAPERBACK ISBN: 978-1-7252-8772-3
HARDCOVER ISBN: 978-1-7252-8773-0
EBOOK ISBN: 978-1-7252-8774-7

01/28/21

To Jane and Martha
and our Parents,
and their parents' ancestors
going back hundreds of thousands of years,
without any of whom
we would not have been here.
And to their innumerable descendants
on many continents and lands
whose other descendants
are our kith and kin today

Contents

Foreword by David P. Gushee | ix

Preface | xiii

Acknowledgements | xix

Introduction | xxi

Part One: Israel's Experience as Immigrants and Refugees | 1

Chapter One: Abraham and Sarai | 3
*Sojourners from Chaldea to Syria, Canaan, Egypt, Canaan and
Syria Again, Then Philistine and Hittite Country,
and Once More, Canaan*

Chapter Two: Isaac and Jacob and Their Families | 7
*Sojourning in Canaan, Philistine Country, Syria,
and Back to Canaan*

Chapter Three: Israel's Long Sojourn in Egypt | 9
Years of Prosperity, Then Oppression

Chapter Four: Israel in the Wilderness:
Another Extended Sojourn | 12

Chapter Five: Back in Canaan Amidst the
Inhabitants of the Land | 16

Chapter Six: At Long Last, a Country
(or Countries) of their Own | 22

Chapter Seven: A House Divided, and the Beginning
of the End of Independence | 25

Chapter Eight: The Decline and Fall of the Two Kingdoms | 27

Chapter Nine: The Exile and Afterwards | 30

Chapter Ten: Review and Preview | 41

Part Two: Sojourners | 47
Biblical Attitudes and Laws Regarding Foreign Immigrants

Chapter Eleven: Marriages and Relations with Foreigners | 49
Positive Viewpoints

Chapter Twelve: Foreign Women, Foreign Gods | 53

Chapter Thirteen: A Nation of Immigrants | 59

Chapter Fourteen: Rights and Interests of Sojourners
and Other Persons in Need | 63

Chapter Fifteen: Foreigners, and Native-Born | 69
All Are Related and All Belong to the LORD

Chapter Sixteen: The Prophets, Israel, and Foreign Nations | 73

Chapter Seventeen: Sojourners Then, and Sojourners Now | 79
Concluding Reflections

Postscript | 85
Bibliography | 87
Index | 91

Foreword

Many American Christians today cite the Bible to support a rejectionist, law-and-order, or #BuildTheWall position in relation to immigrants, especially those illegally crossing our southern border. Sometimes they deploy Romans 13, in which the Apostle Paul calls on Christians to submit to governing authority and its coercive power. Sometimes they talk about the days after the Babylonian Exile in which Nehemiah led the Jewish people in rebuilding the walls of Jerusalem. And sometimes they simply cite the need to trust the wisdom and policymaking of Donald J. Trump, whom they believe to be the God-selected, God-anointed United States president to whom all godly Americans should and will defer.

It sometimes seems hardly worth the effort to engage these claims on their face. Often, they are gossamer-thin veils for sentiments grounded in less holy motivations than a desire to obey God's Holy Word. White supremacism, racism, and xenophobia among white American Christians appear to be surging. Or, at least, surging out into the open, coming out from under the rocks where it had been hiding. This is a time in which the unspeakable is said out loud, and in which the moral restraints provided by the core teaching of Jesus Christ appear to hold little appeal to many who bear a religious identity provided by his name.

In this deceptively brief book, biblical scholar Richard Hiers shows that for half of the long period of biblical history, the Jewish people were sojourners in lands under other people's control. (They were also sojourners for two millennia after that.) The people of God were strangers; visitors; refugees; immigrants; resident aliens; exiles. When they had control of the land they believed to be given to them by God, they remembered their experiences and (at God's command, according to the Bible) created legal and moral codes that demanded compassionate treatment of sojourners and resident aliens. This in turn became one of the most creative and constructive moral legacies of the Hebrew Bible.

The story continues in a different way in the New Testament. Theologically understood, Jesus Christ the Son of God is a visitor, a resident alien, on Earth, in Roman-ruled Palestine, and among his own Jewish people. Under Rome he has no rights and dies a wretched, tortuous death, after a sham trial, on a Roman cross. The Church which Jesus founds and which spreads throughout the Greco-Roman world understands itself as a community of aliens and strangers, just like its Lord. Its true home is a heavenly city that does not yet exist but is coming. While that City is awaited, the Church is a sojourning people.

Most everyone wants to find a home and to feel at home. Most everyone wants their own little spot on earth, to have no one question their ability and right to be there, to enjoy the peace, security, and taken-for-granted at-home-ness of a beloved place. Perhaps most readers of this book have had the good fortune to find a home, and feel at home, like this.

But the hard evidence of history reveals that human beings are often at their worst precisely when they feel very much at home, and then encounter strangers in need at, or within, their borders. *Our* at-home-ness so often seems to depend on *their* rejection. *Our* place is ours only when *they* stay away. The Hebrew Bible's laws about sojourners and resident aliens were designed precisely to prevent the triumph of this kind of thinking. Out of gratitude to God both for sustaining grace during their sojourn times and for the gift of a place of their own, the Jewish people would be a compassionate and welcoming people. They would remember in their bones what it felt like to be refugees, aliens, strangers in need of welcome. They would offer both personal and collective hospitality to those in need. And they would never forget that ultimately all the earth belongs to the Lord and we, all of us, are just passing through. We are all sojourners.

Richard Hiers reminds us of all this by taking us back into the Bible itself—not a prooftext from Romans 13, not a story from Nehemiah, but the main line of the biblical narrative and the heartbeat of biblical law.

Anyone who wants to be "biblical" will begin from a place of compassion toward the sojourners—at our border, in our detention centers, and in our communities. There is much more to say. But that is the first thing to say.

David P. Gushee

Preface

THIS ESSAY BEGAN AS the draft of a new chapter that I intended to add to a second or revised edition of my 2012 book, *Women's Rights and the Bible*. While writing that book, I was surprised to discover that women's status, at least in the Old Testament,[1] was much more elevated than had been generally assumed. And that women's rights in those ancient times occasionally anticipated or paralleled recent advances in modern Anglo-American jurisprudence.

For example, under biblical common or statutory law, women could make contracts; purchase, own or sell real property; be beneficiaries of wills and what now is called inheritance or "intestate succession"; and make bequests or wills devising property to others. In several kinds of situations, women were entitled to some approximation of what in modern American jurisprudence is called "the equal protection of the laws." Several biblical laws called for a variety of compassionate arrangements for providing needy widows and orphans with food.

1. In this essay we use the name "Old Testament" rather than "Hebrew Bible." These two scriptures differ in several significant respects. Among these is the fact that the Christian Old Testament includes several writings not found in the Hebrew Bible. In Protestant Christianity, these writings are designated "Old Testament Apocrypha," but in Catholic and Eastern Orthodox bibles are accorded fully scriptural status. Most of the texts cited here are substantially the same as those found in the Hebrew Bible or *Tanakh*.

But I neglected to include a chapter on the status of foreign women residing in Israel and Judah. Soon it became clear that biblical laws and customs referring to women sojourners also usually applied to men and children. Moreover, it is increasingly obvious that the status and treatment of immigrants in the modern world has become a matter of urgent concern both in the United States and in much of the rest of the world.[2] In this connection, people concerned with treatment of immigrants sometimes refer to the Book of Ruth for support. But few biblical scholars or others focusing on Christian ethics and social policy have recognized the extent to which biblical laws call for protecting the rights and interests of immigrants or resident aliens.[3]

So it seemed timely to look more fully into the attitudes to and treatment of foreigners or resident aliens of all genders in biblical tradition and law. In our earlier book, we found that under biblical law women were, to a considerable extent, treated as a "protected class." In the present essay, we examine ways in which sojourners enjoyed similar and perhaps additional privileges and protections in biblical times.

The present study has led to more surprising findings. One of the striking—though commonly unnoticed—features of biblical law is its repeated insistence on protecting and promoting the rights and well-being of *gerim* (plural for *ger*) translated by such terms as sojourners, refugees,

---

2. See, e.g., Fernandez, "Fight for Asylum." 5–6, and Carter, *Palestine*.

3. See, e.g., Ortiz, "Texas bishops condemn Republican governor." The bishops had rebuked the Texas governor for having barred refugees and failing to "welcome the stranger," The statement evidently was referring to Matthew 25:35, and perhaps to Isaiah 58:17, Hebrews 13:12, or 3 John 9—10. The bishops might also have cited a number of Old Testament texts that relate clearly to foreign sojourners or immigrants. Strangely, sojourners are rarely mentioned in otherwise thorough and excellent books on Old Testament ethics and law, e.g., Green and Lapsley, *Old Testament and Ethics*, Doorly, *Laws of Yahweh*, and Brin, *Studies in Biblical Law*.

asylum-seekers, migrants, strangers, immigrants, or foreigners who were present among the people of Israel and Judah. Several biblical laws applied to native-born and to *gerim*, alike. Some of these laws state explicitly that *gerim* were to enjoy *all* the same legal protections and privileges as native-born members of the community. In effect, *gerim* were another "protected class" of persons who were entitled to enjoy "the equal protection of the laws."

Some later Old Testament writings express negative or hostile attitudes toward foreigners, both those who were residents and those living in foreign nations, and toward foreign nations generally. These attitudes are considered here in the context of basic or core biblical beliefs and understandings about the human condition. These beliefs and understandings are implicitly and often explicitly expressed in a variety of familiar biblical texts.

In the course of thinking and writing about biblical Israel's attitudes and laws regarding *gerim*, I came to realize that Israelites, Judahites, and Jews, themselves, were sojourners or resident aliens in lands owned or controlled by other peoples or nations during the greater part of the biblical period. That experience, or those experiences, clearly contributed to their appreciation of and empathy for foreigners dwelling in their midst as sojourners. Therefore, in Part One of this study we explore the complex history of Israel as a people and sometimes nation of sojourners, from Abraham to the diaspora, or the biblical period between ca. 1800 BCE and 100 CE.

The essay concludes with some reflections on possible parallels between biblical laws and attitudes in regard to the status of sojourners. and modern democratic beliefs and values, particularly as expressed in contemporary American jurisprudence.

Some readers may be puzzled by the emphasis here (and in some of the secondary sources cited) on biblical *law*.

Biblical scholars and moral theologians who are Christian sometimes view Old Testament law with disdain, or ignore it altogether. Statements attributed to both Jesus and Paul can be read as saying either that biblical law was no longer in effect, or, alternatively, that it was "holy, just, and good" and would remain applicable until the end of the age. Recent theologians and commentators sometimes suggest or imply that Old Testament law had to do only with duties (particularly those involving ritual minutiae) that are now considered outmoded, existentially inconsequential, and best abandoned.[4] As if Old Testament law had nothing to say about compassion and social justice.[5] Modernists and post-modernists alike tend to disparage law or any basis for decision-making beyond their own subjective preferences.[6] A timely project for further research by others might be to investigate ways in which classical[7]

---

4. Rudolf Bultmann saw a sharp difference between biblical law, understood as something that had to be obeyed simply because it was commanded (a belief he implicitly attributed to Judaism), and what he called "radical obedience," meaning obedience from the heart, based on love for the other. See Hiers, *Jesus and Ethics*, 79–114. Christian writers sometimes give the impression that they believe love was first invented in the New Testament. Paul Tillich, Dietrich Bonhoeffer, and Karl Barth had little to say about Old Testament law as a basis for modern normative reflection

5. And as if the Old Testament were not Christian scripture. Christian social ethicists only rarely draw upon Old Testament sources when addressing contemporary societal issues. Modern Protestant scholars' tendency to recharacterize the Old Testament as "Hebrew Scriptures" may or may not reflect a wish to disown the Old Testament as Christian scripture.

6. See, e.g., Robert Bellah's account of the difficulty contemporary Americans have when attempting to explain why they sometimes engage in community service or do things for the benefit of others. *Habits of the Heart.* Joseph Fletcher, who confessed (or professed) that he was allergic to law in general, famously declared that people should do whatever "the situation" required, so long as "love is served." Joseph Fletcher, *Situation Ethics.* Antinomian currents have long been recurrent in American culture, which tends to focus on freedom or liberty and less, if at all, on justice.

7. For instance, Augustine, Aquinas, Luther, Calvin, Jonathan Edwards, and John Wesley.

and more recent[8] and contemporary[9] moral theologians have understood or understand biblical law as a resource for normative insight and guidance regarding contemporary issues in ethics and social policy.

Our purpose in this study is to recognize the many biblical passages or texts that pertain to this topic, and to describe what they had to say about it. In order to do so, we often quote biblical texts,[10] sometimes at length, inviting readers to encounter and experience their meanings for themselves. Accordingly, we try not to distract readers by discussing commentaries or other secondary scholarly literature. We do, occasionally, cite other sources and observations in order to provide historical background information or reference to pertinent interpretations and suggestions by others.

Richard H. Hiers
September, 2020

---

8. For instance, Waldo Beach, Robert McAfee Brown, Emil Brunner, William Sloane Coffin, Martin Luther King Jr., Liston Pope, Reinhold Niebuhr, Walter Rauschenbusch, and John Howard Yoder.

9. For instance, , Lisa Sowle Cahill, Stephen L. Carter, James Cone, Charles Curran, Margaret Farley, Pope Francis, David P. Gushee, James M. Gustafson, M. Cathleen Kaveny, Howard Lesnick, David Little, Edward LeRoy Long Jr., Robin W. Lovin, Michael J. Perry, Peter Paris, Donald W. Shriver Jr., Glen H. Stassen, Darryl M. Trimiew. and John Witte Jr.

10. In this essay, Bible quotations generally follow Revised Standard Version translations.

Acknowledgements

I GRATEFULLY ACKNOWLEDGE THE ideas and, sometimes, the language of others whose writings have helped me understand and express my thoughts about the matters considered in this extended essay.

In addition, I wish to express my appreciation to a great many people—more than can be named here—for insights and understandings shared with me during my several decades of sojourning in this world. Some have been teachers and mentors, some fellow students, and former students, others colleagues. They and many other kind friends have encouraged me to continue trying to comprehend the riches and complexities of the human condition. Particularly those related to biblical tradition, to ethics and social ethics, and to law and public policy. All have been helpful in special ways.

Semper sint in flore

Introduction

BEFORE BEGINNING TO EXAMINE Israel's history as sojourners living under foreign rule, and their laws and attitudes as
to foreign sojourners living with them, it may be helpful to
review two preliminary matters. One is the question whether
or the extent to which the biblical stories considered here
should be understood to represent a reliable historical record. The other has to do with the different names by which
the biblical people and nation(s) were known at various
times during the biblical period.

STORY AND HISTORY

Many biblical stories, especially in the early chapters of Genesis, can be read either as actual history, or as legends, that
is, early ways of understanding various phenomena: Such
phenomena as the fact that men and women feel attracted to
one another, and that although neighboring people were like
each other in many ways, they spoke different languages.[1]
Biblical scholars come to differing conclusions as to such
matters as the dating of Abraham and Sarah, or the length
of Israel's sojourn in Egypt. The biblical accounts leave in
question whether that sojourn lasted only a generation or
two. or continued for more than four hundred years. And as

1. See generally, Gunkel, *Legends of Genesis*.

will be seen, it remains unclear whether Israel succeeded in its "conquest" of Canaan, or only managed to occupy some areas, and then, only partially and temporarily.

In this essay we do not attempt to distinguish story from history. That is, we do not try to decide which biblical narratives may reflect some measure of historical (and archeological) accuracy.[2] Or which are better read as creative, albeit sometimes imaginative, efforts to recall past events in order to understand the present and express hopes for the future. Instead, focus in Part One is on ways the people of Israel remembered and understood the experiences of their forebears as sojourners with other peoples as represented in these stories. Then in Part Two we consider biblical attitudes and laws regarding sojourners. We do not attempt to date events precisely. Nor do we try to distinguish particular law codes, or determine which laws might have been set down as early as the time of Moses, and which more likely date from later periods in biblical history.[3]

THE NAME "ISRAEL"

Another preliminary matter: to whom does the name "Israel" refer? Biblical traditions use the name in several different ways. First as the name given by the LORD[4] to Jacob, fol-

---

2. A project undertaken in earlier decades by the late William F. Albright, G. Ernest Wright, John Bright, and many others.

3. Here we use the abbreviation, "ca." (for "circa") to indicate approximate rather than definite dates.

4. In Hebrew texts the divine name is often represented by four letters equivalent in English to the letters YHWH. In traditional Judaism, the name is not to be pronounced, and the four letters are given vowel points from another word (meaning "lord"), which word is to be spoken instead. The four English letters are sometimes pronounced "Yahweh," but here, out of respect for Jewish tradition, we follow the practice of many English translators and use the name "the LORD."

lowing his night-time wrestling with the angel (Gen 32:28).[5] Next, as the name given to Jacob's growing family who, taken together constituted the "Israel" that entered Egypt to buy grain and sojourned there for some time. There, Jacob's family "was fruitful" and had "multiplied" to the extent that, as the story is told, Israel had become so numerous that "the land was filled with them." So much so that their continued presence was no longer welcomed by Egyptian authorities who, after experiencing a series of catastrophic plagues, urgently told them to leave.

Following their subsequent exodus from Egypt,[6] and a long interval of sojourning in "the wilderness," they were commonly known as Israel or Israelites. They were now the people of Israel, but not yet a nation. After entering the land of the Canaanites, they remained a loose confederation of tribes, ruled by a series of charismatic and sometimes effective leaders known as "judges."

In time, perhaps ca. 1000 BCE, a group of northern tribes came together under the leadership of Saul, and for the first time,"Israel" became a a nation, with Saul its first king. Soon afterwards, David, a Judahite, became king over the southern tribe of Judah, which now became the Kingdom of Judah. For some time, the kingdoms of Israel and Judah were at war with each other, but eventually united under David as their king. At this point in the biblical story, the name Israel sometimes refers to this united kingdom, but sometimes, more narrowly, to the people of the former Northern Kingdom who were now subject to David's rule. The two kingdoms remained united under David's son, Solomon, and briefly under Solomon's son, Rehoboam.

---

5. Or an alternative explanation, Gen. 35:10).

6. Known generally as "the Exodus."

But the people of the former Kingdom of Israel, grew restive under the harsh rule of these last two kings and broke away, re-establishing the separate Kingdom of Israel. Again there was war between the kingdoms of Israel and Judah. Following the breakup of the united kingdom, the name, "Israel" generally refers to the Northern Kingdom. This Israel survived until ca. 722 BCE, when it was overrun by Assyria. A great number of its people were then deported into various locations within this powerful empire. The nation or Kingdom of Israel no longer existed.

Now, only Judah[7] remained from what had been the former, briefly united, kingdoms of Israel and Judah. The Southern Kingdom, Judah continued to be ruled by a succession of David's descendants.

In the course of the following century, the people of Judah began to call themselves "Israelites" or "Israel," and to consider themselves heirs to the history and traditions, promises, hopes, and aspirations of the Israelites of earlier times, all of whom, according to biblical accounts, were descended from Abraham and Sarah, and from Jacob,[8] whose name was "Israel."

But then during sixth century, BCE, the Kingdom of Judah was overrun by the neo-Babylonian empire. Many, if not most, of its people were deported or carried away into "exile" in Babylon, and Judah ceased to exist as a nation. Yet in the course of the next hundred years, the name "Israel" again comes to be used, this time referring to the descendants of the people of Judah,[9] who continued to survive for the

7. This separate kingdom may also have included some of the territory, and possibly some of the surviving people from the adjacent northern tribe of Benjamin.

8. And from one or another of Jacob's four wives.

9. At the same time, some of these Israelites also came to be identified as Jews. See, eg., 2 Kgs 25:25; Ezra 4:23; 5:1; 6:7–8; and Nehemiah 4:1.

greater part of the next four centuries as aliens or sojourners in lands dominated by a series of foreign empires: Persian, Greek, Ptolemaic, Seleucid, and Roman.[10]

It is likely that adopting the name Israel served as a way for these latter-day "Israelites" to connect themselves with the larger history, law, culture, and traditions inherited from their ancestors, going all the way back to Abraham and Sarai. In this study, we use the name "Israel" in all of these ways, depending on usages found in texts referring to these respective biblical periods and contexts.

We now turn, in Part One, to an examination of the histories and stories about Israelites as sojourners during the greater part of the long and complicated biblical period. We begin, of course, with stories about Abraham and Sarah, and their immediate descendants.

---

10. Except for the period from ca. 165 to 40 or 39 BCE, when the Jewish people enjoyed some measure of independence under the leadership of the Maccabeans.

Part One

Israel's Experience as Immigrants and Refugees

Chapter One

Abraham and Sarai

Sojourners from Chaldea to Syria, Canaan, Egypt, Canaan and Syria Again, Then Philistine and Hittite Country, and Once More, Canaan

ACCORDING TO GEN 11:24–30, both Abram and Sarah—later known as Abraham and Sarah—were natives of Chaldea (also known as Babylon). Other texts indicate that both, instead, were natives of Aram (also known as Syria).[1] Their initial family connections and countries of origin are considered in later chapters of this study. In any case, as the biblical story is told, they and their extended family moved from Chaldea to Haran, an area located in Syria (Gen 11:31–32). There they settled or sojourned, for the time being. Abraham, of course, was not Israel or an Israelite, but as the biblical account unfolds, he was to become the grandfather of Jacob, who was renamed Israel, and the forefather of all the biblical people of Israel (and Judah), and his wife, Sarah, would be

---

1. In this study, as a convenience, we usually refer to this land, which lay immediately to the north and east of the tribes and later kingdom of Israel, as Syria.

their mother, grand-mother, and foremother.[2] So Abraham's and Sarah's family's migration—or immigration—into Haran could be considered Israel's first experience as sojourners in another land. As will be seen, Abraham's son, Isaac, and grandson, Jacob, also had significant inter-actions with members of the family who lived in Syria.

After some years, as the story continues, "the LORD said to Abraham, 'Go from your country and your kindred and your father's house, to the land that I will show you' " (Gen 12:1). Then follows the LORD's famous promise to Abram: to bless him, to make of him a "great nation," and a blessing to "all the families of the earth." So Abram went, with his family, into Canaan. But as the narrator observes, "At that time the Canaanites were in the land" (Gen 12:4–6). The Canaanites remained in the land for several centuries; during which time, Abraham and his family and their descendants had to cope with their persistent presence, and also the presence of other peoples, notably Hittites and Philistines. As the biblical story is told, Philistines occupied and dominated significant parts of Canaan during the time of Abraham and many of his descendants.[3] Initially, Abraham and his family were sojourners, journeying through, but not yet establishing themselves in the land of the Canaanites.[4]

Soon they had to move on: "Now there was a famine in the land. So Abram went down to Egypt to sojourn there, for

2. Biblical scholars generally agree that the so-called patriarchs and their wives and families lived somewhere between 1800 and 1400 BCE. As to "patriarchs," see below p. 47 n.1.

3. Some biblical historians suggest that the Philistines first appeared in Canaan, along the coastal plain, ca.1200 BCE, about the same time Israelite tribes began to occupy Canaan's central hill areas. As will be noted, Philistines figured prominently in Israel's history during the period of the Judges and the time of Saul and David (ca. 1200 to 1000 BCE).

4. At this point in the narrative, it is said that the LORD told Abraham that he and his descendants would "be sojourners in a land that is not theirs" and there be slaves and oppressed for over four hundred years (Gen 15:13).

the famine was severe in the land" (Gen 12:10). This sojourn and their reason for moving to Egypt foreshadow the subsequent extended sojourn of Jacob and his family (and consequently, all "Israel") in Egypt as described in the last chapters of Genesis and the beginning of Exodus. Abraham and his family prospered in Egypt, for both he and his nephew, Lot, are said to have become very wealthy by the time they left Egypt and returned to Canaan (Gen 13:1–6). Now they again were sojourners in Canaan, for as the narrator reports, "At that time the Canaanites and the Perizzites dwelt in the land" (Gen 13:7). And, as will be seen, the Canaanites were not always glad to welcome these foreign immigrants into their midst.

Canaan, the land of Abraham's sojourning, was the land God promised to him and his descendants as "an everlasting possession" (Gen 17:7–8). Yet Abraham and his family were still on the move. "From there, Abraham journeyed toward the territory of the Negeb, . . . and he sojourned in Gerar," a Philistine city or kingdom (Gen 20:1). And here Abraham and his family sojourned for "many days" (Gen 21:34). Abraham and his descendants would have many more days—and years—of sojourning with, and dwelling under the shadow of the Philistines in the land of Canaan.

Hittites also were in the land at that time. While sojourning in Hittite country, Abraham's wife, Sarah, died, it is said, at the age of one hundred and twenty-seven, having given birth—at the age of ninety—to their son, Isaac. As a sojourner, Abraham had no land of his own, and so turned to his Hittite neighbors for help: "I am a stranger and a sojourner among you: give me the property among you for a burying place, that I may bury my dead out of my sight" (Gen 23:4). During the negotiations that followed, Abraham insists on paying the "full price" for this small piece of land, thereby it seems, under ancient Near Eastern common law, acquiring legal title to it "as a possession" (Gen 23:7–20).[5]

Afterwards, Abraham and his family evidently moved back into Canaanite territory; for in the next chapter, it is said that Abraham dwelled among the Canaanites (Gen 24:3, 37). But Abraham did not want his son, Isaac, to marry any Canaanite women, so he sent his servant to go back to his "country" and his "kindred" in Syria, to find a wife for Isaac there (Gen 24:4). So instructed, the servant travels to the city of Nahor in Syria. Here, the servant encounters Rebekah by a well, and soon meets her brother (and Abraham's nephew), Laban. The servant then takes Rebekah back to Canaan, where she and Isaac are married (Gen 24:10–67).[6]

Sometime later, Abraham died, it is said, at the age of a hundred and seventy-five, and was buried with Sarah in the Cave of Machpelah, the property he had purchased from Ephron, the Hittite (Gen 25:7–11). The narrative now turns to Isaac and his wife, Rebekah, and their family.

---

5. See generally, Westbrook, *Property*.

6. Two incidental details in this story are noteworthy. Rebekah does not go with the servant until she is asked if she would, and had agreed to do so Gen 24:57–58; and it is said that Isaac then not only took her as his wife, but "loved her" (Gen 24:67).

Chapter Two

Isaac and Jacob
and Their Families

Sojourning in Canaan, Philistine Country,
Syria, and Back to Canaan

FOR A WHILE, ISAAC continued to live in the land of Canaan. But soon "there was a famine in the land" and so, like his father, Abraham, under similar circumstances, Isaac and his family moved to the Philistine city of Gerar, and sojourned there (Gen 26:1–11). And like Abraham, he prospered there, to the extent that, as the story is told, the Philistines asked him and has retinue to leave: "Go away from us, for you are much mightier than we" (Gen 26:16). So Isaac and his family and followers moved back to Beersheba, another part of Canaanite territory then occupied by Philistines (Gen 26:17–33). Soon afterwards, Isaac died, but not before mistakenly blessing his son, Jacob, instead of Esau, Jacob's twin brother (Gen 27:1–40).[1] Fearing Esau's vengeance, and instructed by

---

1. At his mother, Rebekah's suggestion, Jacob had come before his blind old father disguised as and pretending to be Esau, his older twin brother. Once

his mother, Rebekah, Jacob fled to Haran, in Syria, in order to take refuge with her brother, Laban (Gen 27:41—28:5). There, the story continues: Jacob marries Laban's two daughters, Rachel and Leah, and also their two handmaidens. Jacob sojourns with his uncle Laban for twenty years, then, no longer feeling welcome, and instructed by the LORD: "Return to the land of your fathers and your kindred,"² Jacob leaves, taking with him his wives, his children, and much of the wealth he had acquired while working for Laban (Gen chapters 30–31).

They return to the land of Canaan. However, the Canaanites were still there, so Jacob and his growing family had to remain sojourners, now in what was supposed to be their own land. Throughout the remainder of the Genesis story, the land remained "the land of Canaan."³ This was still just "the land of their sojourning" (Gen 36:6–7). Summing up "the history of Jacob and his family," the biblical narrator writes: "Jacob dwelt in the land of his father's sojournings, in the land of Canaan" (Gen 37:1). Later, Jacob. himself, now in Egypt, responds to Pharaoh's friendly inquiry as to his age, "The days of the years of my sojourning are a hundred and thirty years" (Gen 47:9). All through their reported lives, Abraham, Isaac, and Jacob and their families were sojourners in other peoples' lands.

It was left to Jacob's son, Joseph, to find himself in a position that led to the people of Israel coming to live as sojourners in Egypt. They did so this time for a few generations, if not centuries, to come.

---

given, it was understood, the blessing could not be withdrawn or transferred.

2. See Gen 31:3.

3. Thus, e.g., Gen 33:18; 34:30; 47:1, 4, 13, 14; 48:3; 50:5, 11, 12. As the Israelites would discover later, it also was the land of other not always friendly peoples or nations. See, e.g., Exod 3:8, 17: Canaanites, Hittites, Amorites, Perizzites, Hivites, and Jebusites. And, most notably, Philistines.

Chapter Three

Israel's Long Sojourn in Egypt

Years of Prosperity, Then Oppression

A PROLONGED PERIOD OF famine in Canaan prompted Jacob to send a delegation of his sons to Egypt, where, he had heard, there was plenty of grain.[1] In Egypt, they find that their younger brother, Joseph, has been installed by the Pharaoh as minister of agriculture in charge of the country's grain conservation and distribution program. Through Joseph's influence, Jacob and his family—now some seventy persons in all—were given land in Goshen, a fertile area in Egypt. There they prospered and "multiplied exceedingly" (Gen 47:27).

They "multiplied and grew [so] exceedingly strong . . . that the land was filled with them." (Exod 1:5-7). In time, they became so many and so strong, as to alarm the new king or pharaoh of Egypt, who feared that "they were "too many

1. "'Why do you look at one another?' And he said, 'Behold, I have heard that there is grain in Egypt; go down and buy grain for us there, that we may live and not die.'" Gen 42:1-2.

and too mighty for us." (Exod 1:9). To deal with their threatening presence, this new king ordered them to do arduous forced labor, in effect, as slaves. And to prevent their further multiplying, he ordered the Egyptian midwives to kill at birth all Israelite children. Israel's sojourn in Egypt now became unbearable.

Moses is introduced in this setting. First as an infant rescued and reared by Pharaoh' daughter; then as a young adult who killed an Egyptian he saw "beating a Hebrew, one of his people" (Exod 2:11–12). Fearing arrest by Egyptian authorities, Moses fled from Egypt and sought refuge in Midian. There he met a Midianite priest named Jethro or Reuel.[2] He married the priest's daughter, Zipporah, and sojourned in Midian. for "many days" or years.[3]

Back in Egypt, the people of Israel "groaned under their bondage." The LORD hears their groaning, appears to Moses (at the burning bush episode), and calls on him to deliver his people from their oppression and suffering in Egypt, and to bring them out of that land, to a "land flowing with milk and honey" (Exod 2:23—3:12). The land was also known as "the place of the Canaanites, the Hittites, the Hivites, and the Jebusites" (Exod 3:8, 17).

Following a series of dramatic encounters with Pharaoh, who consistently refuses to let the people of Israel go, at the LORD's behest, Moses (and his brother Aaron) inflict the Egyptians with a series of frightful plagues (Exod chapters 4–12). Finally, Pharaoh tells Moses and Aaron to leave Egypt, and take with them all the people of Israel and their flocks and herds; just "be gone" (Exod 12:31–32). According

2. Exodus 2:15–22; Num 10:29.

3. Exodus 2:22–23. Long enough for Moses and Zipporah to have had and raised some number of sons. Exod 4:20.

to Exod 12:40, "The time that the people of Israel [had] dwelt in Egypt was four hundred and thirty years."[4] Moses leads them out of Egypt, and in perhaps the most vivid of all biblical scenarios, through the middle of the Red Sea, which then surges back, drowning Pharaoh's pursuing army.[5] This amazing escape is celebrated in the dramatic Song (or psalm) of Moses (Exod 15:1–18).[6] Moses' next task was to bring the people of Israel to the promised land, the land of the Canaanites—and other resident peoples or nations. In order to get there, they had to traverse a great wilderness that lay between Egypt and Canaan.

4. It might be inferred from Exod 1:1–9 that Israel's sojourn in Egypt extended for only a generation or two.

5. Exodus 14:5–31. Historians of the period offer many theories as to what actually may have happened, and about such geographical questions as the location of the "Red Sea" (or "Sea of Reeds.)" For purposes of this study, it is enough to focus on the biblical accounts as later remembered and set down. Apart from what actually may have occurred, these remembered stories provided the basis for Israel's later reflections on their experiences as immigrants. And, as will be seen in Part Two, affected their attitudes and laws regarding foreign immigrants.

6. In the Song of Miriam, Moses' sister, Miriam also was regarded as a prophet (Exod 15:20–21). It may well be that the Song of Moses should have been attributed to Miriam. See Trible, *Eve and Miriam*, 5–24.

Chapter Four

Israel in the Wilderness

Another Extended Sojourn

THE STORY—OR MORE PROPERLY, stories—of Israel's jour-
ney through the wilderness begins in Exod 16:1, continues
through the Books of Leviticus, Numbers, and Deuteronomy,
and concludes with an account of Moses' death and burial in
Moab (Deut 34:5–8). These stories recount the people's journeying and sojourneying in many wilderness areas within
what is now known as the Sinai Peninsula. The Hebrew title
for the Book of Numbers is simply "In Wilderness." Following sometimes uncertain clues in the texts of these four
biblical books, map-makers have tried to trace Israel's possible routes through this wilderness, or these wildernesses,
and the particular places where they may have sojourned
along the way. Here, however, we are concerned only with
their experiences as remembered in biblical tradition. As a
convenience, in the following discussion, we refer simply to
"the wilderness," rather than any particular wildernesses or
routes the Israelites may have taken.

One notable feature of these stories is the candor with which the narrators report the people of Israel's bitter complaints about being brought from the comforts of life in Egypt into this desolate wilderness. Understandably trembling before Pharaoh's approaching army (which was pursuing them after their departure, but before the Red Sea event), the people of Israel exclaim to Moses:

> Is it because there are no graves in Egypt that you have taken us away to die in the wilderness? What have you done to us, in bringing us out of Egypt? Is not this what we said to you in Egypt; 'Let us alone and let us serve the Egyptians?' For it would have been better for us to serve the Egyptians than to die in the wilderness.[1]

Then having safely arrived in the Sinai wilderness after the Red Sea episode, the people again complain, this time about lack of food. For example, in Exod 16:2–3:

> And the whole congregation of the people of Israel murmured against Moses and Aaron in the wilderness, and said to them, 'Would that we had died . . . in the land of Egypt, when we sat by the fleshpots and ate bread to the full; for you have brought us out into this wilderness to kill this whole assembly with hunger.'

In response, the LORD gave them manna for food;[2] and then when they complained about that,[3] threatened to give them so much they would choke on it.[4] And then finally sent them meat to eat.[5]

---

1. Exodus 14:11–12.
2. Exodus 16:13–31.
3. Numbers 11:4: "'O that we had meat to eat! We remember the fish we ate in Egypt for nothing, the cucumbers, the melons, the leeks, the onions, and the garlic. But now our strength is dried up, and there is nothing at all but this manna to look at.'"
4. Numbers 11:18–20.
5. Numbers 11:31–32.

The most important feature of the wilderness era was that, according to the tradition, it was here that the LORD— with Moses as mediator and spokesman—gave Israel the Law. In subsequent Jewish tradition, all five of the first books of the Bible are called the "Torah," meaning God's instruction or law.

It may be noted that Israel's experience of receiving the Law was remembered as having taken place shortly after being freed from bondage in Egypt. Back in Egypt, they had been subject to Egyptian law. Now that they were free, how should their lives be governed? How to balance rights and responsibilities, in ways that were fair and just? The American experience was similar: after becoming free from England's rule, and a brief and chaotic experience under the "Articles of Confederation," the Founders moved quickly to put together a constitution (*the Constitution*), to provide the necessary framework for the new nation's evolving legal system.[6]

Large portions of the books of Exodus, Leviticus, Numbers, and Deuteronomy consist of laws and ordinances ordained by the LORD, for Israel to observe forever. Many of these laws concern rituals and ceremonies, some involving sacrificial offerings, detailing when, where, how, and by whom they were to be carried out.[7] Many other laws have to do with relations between and among persons in the community of Israel, and their obligations to and responsibilities for each other and for the welfare of the people and nation as a whole. Biblical law-givers seem to have recognized that

6. See generally, Dahl, *After the Revolution*. Similarly, the Napoleonic Code followed soon after the French Revolution. The U.S. Constitution was expected to evolve, as can be seen by the fact that it included provisions for amendment as time goes by and new concerns come to light. Biblical law also evolved, as can be seen in the fact that laws in some codes amend provisions in earlier codes. See Hiers, *Justice and Compassion*.

7. Several of these laws are discussed by the present author in "Reverence for Life."

freedom without laws protecting those who were vulnerable and defining the obligations of the more powerful, would be certain to result in oppression rather than social justice.[8] The substance of these laws need not detain us here, but as will be seen in Part Two of this essay, several of them appear to have been inspired by and drawn from the people's recollection of their forebears' experience as sojourners in foreign lands.

Numbers chapter 33 summarizes the "stages" of the people's sojourning in the wilderness, from the time they "went forth out of the land of Egypt . . . under the leadership of Moses and Aaron" (Num 33:1), until the time they gathered in Moab and began making ready to "pass over the Jordan into the land of Canaan" (Num 33:41–53). It is said that Israel sojourned in the wilderness for forty years.[9]

Before Moses' death, the LORD gave instructions as to how the land of Canaan was to be divided or apportioned among the tribes of Israel.[10] But he also cautioned that the people of Israel would have to drive out the "inhabitants of the land." "[For] those of them whom you let remain shall be as pricks in your eyes and thorns in your sides, and they shall trouble you in the land where you dwell" (Num 33:55). It would remain for Joshua, and later, the "judges" of Israel, to discover how difficult the task of driving out the land's inhabitants would prove to be.

---

8. Many of these laws concerned what might now be called "social ethics," or 'ethics and public policy" issues. See Westbrook and Wells, *Everyday Law,* and Hiers, *Justice and Compassion.*

9. Numbers 3:38; Josh 5:6; Amos 5:25.

10. Numbers chapter 34.

Chapter Five

Back in Canaan Amidst
the Inhabitants of the Land

THE WILDERNESS ERA WAS over; yet the people of Israel, now camping or sojourning in Moab, just east of the Jordan River, had yet to enter the "promised land," which was still the land of Canaan. At the beginning of the story as told in the Book of Joshua, "the LORD said to Joshua, 'Moses, my servant is dead; now therefore arise, go over this Jordan, you and all this people. into the land which I am giving them, to the people of Israel" (Josh 1:2).

For a brief period, Israelites continued to sojourn in Moab. During this time Joshua sent two spies to "view" the land they were about to enter (Josh 2:1). The men came to Jericho, where they were sheltered by Rahab, "the harlot." After they reported back to Joshua, he proceeded to lead the Israelites' across the Jordan River. Again, the LORD re-assures the people that he would, "without fail drive out from before you the Canaanites, the Hivites, the Hittites, the Perizzites, the Gergashites, the Amorites, and the Jebusites"

(Josh 3:10).[1] In the same way that Israel had previously gone straight through the Red Sea after leaving Egypt, the people of Israel again pass right through water, this time the Jordan River (Josh 3:11—4:24).

The stories that follow describe how the people of Israel defeated and slaughtered the land's inhabitants, beginning with those at Jericho and Ai (Josh chapters 6–8).[2] Possibly forgetting that they (and the LORD) were merely meant to drive these inhabitants out from the land, these stories repeatedly say that the Israelites "slaughtered" or "utterly destroyed" all the inhabitants of each town or village, leaving none alive.[3]

The story of Israel's military activities during this period is sometimes referred to as their "conquest" of Canaan. A number of texts suggest that this term might be appropriate. For instance, Josh 11:16: "So Joshua took all that land, the hill country and all the Negeb and all the land of Goshen and the lowland and the Arabah and the hill country of Israel and its lowland . . ."[4]

Nevertheless, it appears that the "conquest" was far from complete. According to Josh 11:22, some of the original inhabitants "remained" in the land; notably in the Philistine cities of Gaza, Gath, and Ashdod. Moreover, the narrator adds, when "Joshua was old and advanced in years, the LORD said to him, '. . . [T]here remains yet very much land to be possessed. This is the land that yet remains: all the regions of the Philistines, and all those of the Geshurites . . .'" A great many

---

1. See also Exod 34:11.

2. The narrator adds that the male Israelites first had to be circumcised, since all of those who had sojourned in the wilderness had died, and those born in the wilderness had not yet been circumcised. Josh 5:2–8. Later descriptions of battle scenes indicate that by this time, the people of Israel were thought to have numbered several thousand—all born in the wilderness.

3. For example, Josh 6:21; 8:22–24; 10:10–12, 20–40; and 11:8, 21.

4. See also Josh 11:21, 23.

of the other previous inhabitants also remained, according to Josh 13:1–6.[5] As to these, the LORD, again promises that he, himself, would "drive them out from before the people of Israel'" (Josh 13:6).

However, Israel's continued presence, even in the places they had managed to occupy, was said to be uncertain, and contingent upon their remaining faithful to the LORD:

> "For if you turn back, and join the remnants of these nations left here among you, and make marriages with them, so that you marry their women and they yours, know assuredly that the LORD your God will not continue to drive them out before you; but they shall be a snare and a trap for you, a scourge on your sides, and thorns in your eyes, till you perish from off the good land which the LORD your God has given you."[6]

As the story proceeds in the Book of Judges, it becomes ever more apparent that Israel's tenure on even part of the land of Canaan was, at best, tenuous.

The Book of Judges begins by summarizing a series of Israelite victories over many of the land's inhabitants: Canaanites, Perizzites, Jerusalem, Zephath (Hormah), Gaza, Ashkelon, Ekron, their surrounding territories, the central hill country, Hebron, and Bethel, the Hittite city of Luz (Judg 1:4–26). At the same time, the narration acknowledges that previous inhabitants remained in a great many places, despite Israelite attempts to destroy or dislodge them.[7] Why? Because, the LORD explains, the Israelites "'have not obeyed my commandments. . . . So now I say, I will not drive them

---

5. See also Josh 13:13.

6. Joshua 23:12–13.

7. See Judg 1:19 Canaanites (explaining that they had "chariots of iron"); Judg 1:21 Jebusites, (the people of Jerusalem); and those in many other places named in Judg 1:27–35 (adding that "later" some or all of those people would be subjected to "forced labor").

out before you; but they shall become adversaries to you . . .'" (Judg 2:2–3).

The narrator organizes the rest of the Judges stories in accordance with the following cyclical pattern: The people of Israel have successfully occupied the land, and now serve the LORD. But then they do evil by worshiping Baals, Ashteroth, or their neighbors' other gods and goddesses. So the LORD gives them back into the hands of their enemies, who plunder and otherwise oppress them. The LORD then hears their cries or groans, has pity on them, and "raises up" a "judge" who delivers them from these enemies, and everything goes well for a while. Until the judge dies, after which the people of Israel again turn to worship foreign gods, and the cycle goes around again.[8] Therefore, he declares, "I will not henceforth drive out before them any of the nations that Joshua left when he died, that by them I may test Israel, whether they will take care to walk in the way[9] of the LORD as their fathers did, or not" (Judg 2:21–22). This theory or theology of history provides the framework for most of the remaining accounts in Judges.[10] Thus the "judges" are said to have succeeded one another as rulers over all Israel, each doing so for some time, but after each judge dies, the people again fail the test and revert to their evil ways. Perhaps this theory was meant to explain why so many (if not all) of the other peoples or nations persisted in dwelling in the land of Canaan. Thus

8. See Judg 2:6–16. Some of the judges are mentioned only in passing, and not fitted into this cycle. For instance: Tola, Jair, Ibram, and Abdon.

9. "Walk in the way" meant to "conduct themselves."

10. This interpretation of events in Judges is sometimes attributed to a Deuteronomic editor (or editors), thought to have collected, organized, and edited the accounts sometime during the seventh or sixth centuries, BCE. The underlying theme in these stories was the message for later people of Israel and Judah: Worship the LORD and no other gods. This was also the fundamental requirement set out at the beginning of the Ten Commandments. And also the core message of most of the Old Testament prophets.

Judges 3:5 explains: "So the people of Israel dwelt among the Canaanites, the Hittites, the Amorites, the Perizzites, the Hivites, and the Jebusites."

For purposes of the present study, it is not necessary to review the series of judges and their accomplishments,[11] or other events that were part of this chaotic period. It may suffice to note that as the story unfolds, Israelites periodically engage in civil wars, and (mainly losing) battles with other peoples, and become involved in gruesome stories of rape, murder, the virtual annihilation of the Israelite tribe of Benjamin, more murder, and kidnapping.[12] The final story line in Judges sums it all up: "In those days there was no king in Israel; every man did what was right in his own eyes" (Judg 21:25).[13] Absent shared commitment to a transcendent center or source of meaning, value, and authority, relationships among the people of Israel, and concern for what was to have been their common good, had largely degenerated into chaos and anarchy.

By the end of the period of the judges,[14] it was clear that Israel's "conquest" of the land of Canaan had failed. The stories about Samson's exploits demonstrate that whatever earlier victories the people Israel might have gained, the Philistines were now their overlords. "At that time, the Philistines had dominion over Israel" (Judg 14:4). Following some of Samson's terrorist acts against Philistines,[15] three thousand men

11. A few of the judges were remembered as very important figures in the over-all history of Israel: for instance, Deborah, the only judge depicted as functioning in a judicial capacity, and Gideon and Jephthah, as famous warriors.

12. See Judg 8:1—21:23.

13. Cf. Deut 12:8.

14. Biblical scholars generally date this period between 1200 and 1000 BCE.

15. Judges 14:38—15:8. The narrator writes that these acts (or some of them) were inspired by "the Spirit of the LORD" coming on Samson (Judg 14:19), but the stories themselves suggest that Samson was inspired more by desire to carry out a personal vendetta. Judg 15:3, 11. The biblical Samson was

of Judah came and pled with him: "'Do you not know that the Philistines are rulers over us? What then is this that you have done to us?'" (Judg 15:11). Notwithstanding Samson's further attacks, including his suicidal destruction of a house or temple full of Philistine men and women (Judg16:23–30), the Philistines continued to dominate Israel.

And did so for a long time afterwards. So complete was this domination that a generation later, when Israelites needed to sharpen their farm implements, they had to ask Philistines to do it for them:

> Now there was no smith to be found throughout all the land of Israel; for the Philistines said, 'Lest the Hebrews make themselves swords or spears'; but every one of the Israelites went down to the Philistines to sharpen his ploughshare, his mattock, his axe, or his sickle, and the charge was a pim for the ploughshares and for the mattocks, and a third of a shekel for sharpening the axes and for setting the goads.[16]

For much of the period of the Judges, it appears that Israelites were still sojourners in the midst of other nations. There was no king, and no kingdom of Israel. Not yet.

---

no "Christ-figure."

16. 1 Sam 13:19–2. In this connection, it may be noted that the judge Ehud had to make his own sword in order to assassinate a Moabite king (Judg 3:16); that judge Shamgar's weapon was an ox goad (Judg 3:31); and at one point, Samson's was the jawbone of an ass (Judg 15:15–17).

Chapter Six

At Long Last, a Country (or Countries) of their Own

SOMETIME AROUND 1000 BCE, a man of great stature and courage named Saul, from the northern tribe of Benjamin, arose to lead a group of fellow Israelites to rescue the nearby Israelite town of Jabesh-Gilead, which had been besieged by Philistines. Their victory led some other northern tribes (and the prophet Samuel) to make Saul king over what came be called Israel.[1] Under Saul's leadership, the people of Israel gained other victories against Philistines, and established, at last, an independent nation of their own.

David, a Judahite, joined Saul's forces, and soon achieved a large popular following for slaying huge numbers of Philistines. Saul, suspecting that David intended to take over his throne, attempted to kill him, but David escaped, and took refuge (or sojourned) with—of all people—the Philistines.[2]

---

1. 1 Samuel 11:12–15. This new kingdom did not include the people or territory of Judah.

2. Some Philistines also wondered what David was doing there. 1 Sam 21:10–15; 27:1–12; 29:1–11.

He pretended to be fighting for them, but instead was sending spoils of battle to the elders of his native Judah as "a present."[3] Soon afterwards, "the men [of Judah] . . . anointed David king over the house of Judah" (2 Sam 2:1–4).

After Saul was killed fighting Philistines, David hinted to the elders of Israel that they should consider making him their king, too.[4] Having fallen out with Saul, Samuel had already anointed David as king of Israel (1 Sam 16:1–13). But the people of Israel were not yet ready to accept this Judahite as their king. Instead: "There was a long war between the house of Saul and the house of David" (2 Sam 3:1). Eventually, "all the tribes of Israel came to David" and anointed him "king over Israel."[5] It is said that David "reigned over all Israel and Judah . . . thirty-three years" (2 Sam 5:4–5).

At last, all Israel—or more precisely, the Northern Kingdom of Israel and the Southern Kingdom of Judah—came together as one nation. The people's long sojourns under Canaanite, Egyptian, Canaanite (again), and Philistine dominion were now over. No longer sojourners, the people of Judah and Israel at last lived in their own country. With the exception of intermittent (and sometimes major) outbreaks of war and civil war,[6] they continued do so during the remainder of David's reign as king, and that of his son, Solomon.[7] This era is commonly referred to as the period of the "United Monarchy."

3. 1 Samuel 30:26–31.

4. 2 Samuel 2:5–7.

5. 2 Samuel 5:1–3. For purposes of this study, it is unnecessary to detail the series of complex intrigues, wars and murders that contributed to this result.

6. For instance: when David's son, Absalom, revolted against his father's rule, and was joined by Israelites in a war against David (2 Sam 15:1—18:33); another war by Israelites against David, this time led by Sheba, a Benjaminite (2 Sam 19:41—20:2); and more wars with Philistines (2 Sam 21:15–22).

7. However, Solomon treated his Israelite subjects as second class citizens, if not slaves or serfs, thereby prompting dangerous resentment that would

Solomon was famed for his wisdom, wealth, and many wives (and concubines), and credited with building and elaborately furnishing the Jerusalem Temple and several royal palaces[8] And also for writing what became three books of the Bible.[9] His reign was celebrated and remembered as the time when: "Judah and Israel were as many as the sand by the sea; they ate and drank and were happy" (1 Kgs 4:20). But this happy era and the United Kingdom would soon come to their end.

---

soon have serious consequences for the people of both former kingdoms.

8. 1 Kings 5:1—7:61.

9. The Song of Solomon, Proverbs, and the Wisdom of Solomon. Cf. 1 Kgs 4:32. He was also noted for his scientific interests (1 Kgs 4:33–34). Solomon was also remembered negatively, for joining his foreign wives in worshiping their foreign deities.

Chapter Seven

A House Divided, and the Beginning of the End of Independence

SOLOMON'S SON, REHOBOAM, INHERITED his father's throne, and assumed the right to absolute rule. He did so harshly, requiring his Israelite subjects to do forced labor. Jeroboam, spokesman for the Israelite labor forces. went before Rehoboam, along with "all the assembly of Israel" and asked him to ease their burdens.[1] Rehoboam arrogantly replied as follows: "My father made you yoke heavy, but I will add to your yoke; my father chastised you with whips, but I will chastise you with scorpions'" (1 Kgs 12:2–14).[2] As might have been expected, the people of Israel responded by breaking away from this would-be tyrant, and going back to having a separate kingdom of their own: "'What portion have we in David? We have no inheritance in the son of Jesse. To your tents, O Israel! Look now to your own house, David.'

1. 1 Kings 12:1–5.
2. Cf. Sir 47:23.

So Israel departed to their tents" (1 Kgs 12:16). Perhaps two centuries later, a commentator, writing from a southern or Judahite perspective, added: "So Israel has been in rebellion against the house of David to this day" (1 Kgs 12:19).

Even though Israel and Judah were often at war in the years that followed the break-up, their people at least lived in their own countries. Judah continued to be governed by David's descendants; while Israel was ruled by kings from several different dynasties. Historians date the break-up of the United Monarchy around 926 BCE. The next two centuries were marked by numerous wars, in which Israel and Judah sometimes allied themselves with other nations or peoples against each other, and occasionally joined together against common enemies. This tumultuous era concluded with the rise of Assyria, which was emerging as the major power in the ancient Near Eastern world.

Chapter Eight

The Decline and Fall
of the Two Kingdoms

ASSYRIA WAS MOVING SLOWLY into the coastal regions east
of the Mediterranean Sea. Around 853 BCE, Assyrian forces
came so near that the three small nations of Syria, Israel, and
Judah, took time off from fighting each another, and formed
a temporary alliance that succeeded in checking Assyrian
advance for more than a century. But then in 722 BCE, the
Assyrian axe fell on the Kingdom of Israel.

Apparently Assyrian policy was to deport the entire
populace of conquered countries to other locations within
their empire. In any case, that is what Assyria now did with
the people of Israel. So the Northern Kingdom, the Kingdom
of Israel, no longer existed. Wherever their people were tak-
en, they no longer lived in or on their own land. They were
now permanent exiles, living, of necessity, as involuntary
sojourners in another land. This deportation was the first of
several which, together, marked the beginning of what later

would be called the diaspora. What may have become of the former population of Israel remains largely unknown.[1]

Almost miraculously, Judah was spared a similar fate two decades later, ca. 701 BCE, when Assyrian king Sennacherib's powerful army was encamped around the very gates of Jerusalem. But for some reason or other, the Assyrian forces quietly withdrew.[2] Judah remained an independent nation for another hundred years. But in the meantime, the neo-Babylonian empire was ominously expanding.[3]

In order to avoid destruction at their hands ca. 598 BCE, the king of Judah was compelled to hand over "all the treasures of the house of the LORD, and the treasures of the king's house" to Nebuchadnezzar, the Babylonian king, The Babylonians also deported "all Jerusalem," including the king and his family, military personnel. and those craftsmen and smiths who were "strong and fit for war."[4] Judah now became a vassal state. A few years later, a number of Judah's leaders tried to re-assert their independence, prompting the Babylonians to lay siege to Jerusalem. Finally, ca. 586 BCE, Babylonian armies entered Jerusalem, destroyed the Temple, burned the city, and deported its leaders and many, if not most of the remaining people of Judah to Babylon.[5]

---

1. Post-biblical references to "the lost ten tribes of Israel" appear to be grounded more on legend than historical evidence. Some scholars have suggested that descendants of Israelites may have escaped from Assyria and later became part of the people known as Samaritans.

2. 2 Kings chapters 18–19. Biblical tradition, *Assyrian Annals*, the ancient historian, Herodotus, and the *Encyclopedia Britannica* offer differing theories.

3. Babylonian forces over-ran the Assyrian capitol, Nineveh, ca.612 BCE.

4. 2 Kings 24:1–21. These events are commonly referred to as the first deportation.

5. A few survivors tried to get help from Egypt, and attempted to overthrow Babylonian rule, but having failed, fled to Egypt (2 Kgs 25:22–46). Again some Israelites were sojourners in Egypt, this time as asylum-seekers.

These events constituted the beginning of what is called the Babylonian exile, or simply, the exile.[6]

6. 2 Kings 24:20—25:21.

Chapter Nine

The Exile and Afterwards

THE PEOPLE OF JUDAH, like those of Israel before them, were now exiles, sojourning, of necessity, in a foreign land. This was the second major episode adding to the diaspora, a term referring to the growing numbers of former Israelites, Judahites, and Jews sojourning in other people's lands.

It was a bitter experience for the exiles, as attested in Psalm 137:

> By the waters of Babylon, there we sat down and wept, when we remembered Zion.[1] . . . How shall we sing the LORD's song in a foreign land? If I forget you, O Jerusalem, let my right hand wither![2]

Little is actually known about the life of the exiles in Babylon. However, there is no indication that they were required to do forced labor—unlike the experience of Israelites during the latter days of their sojourn in Egypt (or later, under the oppressive rule of Solomon and Rehoboam). In

---

1. Meaning Jerusalem, or sometimes, specifically, the Jerusalem Temple.
2. Psalm 137:1, 4–5.

his letter to the exiles, Jeremiah channels the LORD's en-
couragement and advice to the Babylonian exiles:

> Thus says the LORD of hosts, the God of Israel, to all
> the exiles whom I have sent into exile from Jerusalem to
> Babylon: "Build houses, and live in them; plant gardens
> and eat their produce. Take wives and have sons and
> daughters, take wives for your sons and give your daugh-
> ters in marriage, that they may bear sons and daughters;
> multiply there, and do not decrease. But seek the welfare
> of the city where I have sent you into exile, and pray to
> the LORD on its behalf, for in its welfare you will find
> your welfare."[3]

A good many exiles must have followed such advice, for
after their subsequent liberation by the Persian King Cyrus,
substantial numbers of them chose to remain in Babylon,
and apparently flourished there. It was here that what would
become one of the most important collections of rabbinical
commentary on the *Torah* was set down and preserved: the
Babylonian Talmud. Perhaps these voluntary sojourners, like
the Israelites in the early years of their voluntary sojourning
in Egypt, were well treated and allowed to prosper.

UNDER PERSIAN RULE

The Persian empire was now expanding and becoming the
dominant power in the ancient Near Eastern world. Unlike his earlier royal counterparts in Assyria and Babylonia,
Cyrus, the Persian emperor (or king), made it his practice
to allow captive peoples to return to their native soils. So,
ca. 539/38 BCE, Cyrus issued his famous decree, allowing
Judahite exiles to return to what had been their homeland in

---

3. Jeremiah 29:4–7.

Jerusalem and Judah.[4] Many did return.[5] And soon afterwards, in 515 BCE, rebuilt the Temple. Under Persian, rule the people of Israel were granted a semi-autonomous way of life. As can be learned from the Books of Ezra and Nehemiah, Persians appointed native, that is, Jewish, leaders as officials, perhaps as governors, to oversee this portion of their empire. Nehemiah and Ezra were the most prominent of those officials. Under Nehemiah's dynamic leadership, Jerusalem's walls and gates were rebuilt in 444 BCE. Jews were now free to practice their religious traditions. Ezra is sometimes credited for codifying a major portion of the laws recorded in Exodus, Leviticus and Numbers. Nehemiah and Ezra undertook vigorously to enforce compliance with the Law or *Torah*. During the Persian period, the Jewish people were no longer involuntary sojourners in other people's lands. Now, at least, they were sojourners in what once had been their own country, even if still living under foreign rule.

This pattern continued for nearly three centuries afterwards. During these years, the Jewish people were ruled by a series of foreigners, as one Near Eastern empire succeeded another. Not much is known about the life of the former exiles and their descendants during the next few centuries.

UNDER GREEK DOMINION AND THE INFLUENCE OF HELLENISTIC CULTURE

The Persian period ended in 331 BCE, when armies of Alexander the Great annexed what had been the land of Israel and its Jewish inhabitants, adding it and them to his now

---

4. The prophet usually designated as Second Isaiah, spoke or wrote of Cyrus as carrying out the LORD's redeeming intent, even suggesting that Cyrus was to be regarded as Messiah. Isa 45:1–6.

5. As noted above, many others evidently chose to remain in Babylonia.

dominant Greek or Hellenistic empire. During this time and for some centuries afterwards Hellenistic culture significantly impacted Jewish society.

UNDER PTOLOMAIC AND SELEUCID RULE; THEN THE MACCABEAN ERA OF FREEDOM

A few years after Alexander's death in 301 BCE, his empire was divided among others. Two of his former generals, and their descendants ruled over the Jewish people, in turn, for more than a century. First, the Ptolomies based in Egypt to the south and east, from ca. 301 to 198 BCE, and then the Seleucids[6] to the north and west, from 198 to ca.165 BCE.

Not much is known about the life of the Jewish people during the Ptolomaic period. More information is available about their experience during the Seleucid era.

Soon after his accession to power in 175 BCE, the new Seleucid king, Antiochus IV ("Epiphanes"), moved against "Israel," over-ran Jerusalem, desecrated the Temple, and—in order that all the people in his empire "should be one people and . . . each should give up his customs"[7]—vigorously undertook to abolish Jewish religious practices. The Jewish people responded by revolting against Seleucid domination. They were led initially by Judas Maccabaeus, his brothers, and later by other members of his family. The years during which Judas and his family led the Jewish struggle for freedom from Seleucid power are known as the Maccabean or Hasmonean era, ca. 167 to 39 BCE. By ca. 142 BCE, Jews had

6. Named for Alexander's former generals: Ptolomy and Seleucus, who gained control over these portions of what had been Alexander's extensive empire.

7. 1 Maccabees 1:20–64. We might see here an early version of the "melting pot" ideal later popular in the United States, according to which immigrants come from all parts of the world, go into the "melting pot," and then are supposed to come out just like "us," i.e., the dominant part of the population.

managed to establish a quasi-independent state that endured for another hundred years.

During those years Jews engaged in many battles, and entered into a series of complex alliances and intrigues with neighboring peoples. Notwithstanding defeats, betrayals and other set-backs, they succeeded in re-gaining control of Jerusalem and some adjacent land. The most important religious moment was when they cleansed and re-dedicated the Temple, ca. 164 BCE (1 Macc 4:43–59). This event was celebrated as "the festival of lights," and is the basis for the later holiday known as Hanukkah. The books of First and Second Maccabees are the principal biblical sources of information about events and Jewish people's experiences and concerns during the Maccabean period.[8]

HELLENISTIC INFLUENCES DURING SELEUCID AND MACCABEAN TIMES

Several other biblical writings probably were composed during the years between Alexander's annexation of Judah (or Judea) and the close of the Maccabean period. Most of these suggest that they were written far back in the days of Babylonian rule. Viewed together, these writings present and exemplify three significant aspects of Jewish life and experience during the Seleucid and Maccabean years. Notably: the growing influence of Hellenistic culture on Jewish beliefs and practices; periodic persecution of Jews who remained faithful to their religious traditions; and recurring temptation, if not compulsion, to worship the "heathen" gods and godlings of their pagan neighbors.

8. The writings of the first century BCE Jewish historian, Josephus, offer additional information and interpretation. Fourth Maccabees might be considered another source, focusing on heroic and tragic experience during those stormy years.

The most obvious evidence of the effect of Hellenistic culture (or Hellenism) on Judaism was the of translation of the Hebrew Bible into Greek. The translation process began ca. 200 BCE, and continued into the first or even second centuries CE, resulting in the production of what became known as the Greek Bible or Septuagint.[9] The Septuagint included the books and other writings found in Hebrew versions, along with others that may have been composed originally in Greek. The translation was thought necessary and desirable because Greek was becoming the *lingua franca* throughout the Mediterranean world. That world was then home to many diaspora Jews who, like their Gentile neighbors, commonly wrote and spoke in Greek.[10]

Not all Jews embraced Hellenism. The author of 2 Maccabees strongly disapproved of high Priest Jason's infatuation with Greek culture:

> [W]hen . . . he came to office, he at once shifted his countrymen over to the Greek way of life. . . . [H]e destroyed the lawful ways of living and introduced new customs contrary to the law. For with alacrity he founded a gymnasium . . . and he induced the noblest of the young men to wear the Geeek hat. There was such an extreme of Hellenization and increase in the adoption of foreign ways . . . that the priests were no longer intent upon their service at the altar. Despising the sanctuary and neglecting the sacrifices, they hastened to take part in the unlawful proceedings in the wrestling arena after the call of the discus . . . [A]nd [put] the highest value upon Greek forms of prestige.[11]

9. Actually there were several somewhat differing versions of the Septuagint.

10. Greek language and culture also influenced Judaism and Christianity in the early centuries CE.

11. 2 Maccabees 4:10–15.

Other aspects of Greek culture were regarded more positively. In particular, the appropriation of philosophical concepts, which were used to understand and reinterpret core Jewish beliefs and understandings. The most notable example is 4 Maccabees,[12] where the writer identifies and virtually equates the Torah with "reason," and characterizes Judaism as a "philosophy." The writer explains that by using reason, fellow Jews can and should control their emotions. The writer apparently intended to represent Judaism in a way that could be understood and accepted by his Hellenistic contemporaries. Somewhat similarly, The Book of Baruch associates, if not equates wisdom with the Law or Torah,[13] and urges readers to recognize wisdom as guide to right living in a wide range of situations or contexts (Bar 3:9–44).[14] Baruch may have been a contemporary of Philo of Alexandria,[15] who likewise presented Judaism as a philosophy and, using an allegorical method of interpretation, believed he could find many elements of Greek philosophy in the Greek Bible.

PERIODIC PERSECUTION

Another prominent feature of Jewish experience during the Seleucid/Maccabean period was persecution. Several biblical writings reflect that experience, some directly, like First and Second Maccabees. Others do so indirectly, by including details suggestive of actions and events known from other

---

12. 4 Maccabees did not gain full canonical status, but is included as an appendix in Greek Orthodox bibles.

13. "She [wisdom] is the book of the commandments of God, and the law that endures forever." Bar 4:1.

14. Cf. the motto of the American Phi Beta Kappa Society: "Love of Wisdom is the guide to life."

15. Ca. 20 BCE to 59 CE.

sources to have occurred in days of Antiochus Epiphanes.[16] Some stories implicitly call for active resistance. For example, the fantastic story about the mad king Ptolemy Philopator's determination to destroy all Jews, found in 3 Maccabees. Or the story of Judith in the book named for her. Others report (or recommend) a variety of inspiring responses to persecution or the prospect of persecution. Notably Daniel, Bel and the Dragon, The Prayer of Azariah, Esther and Additions to Esther, and 4 Maccabees. Such persecutions may have been prompted by Jews' resistance to invasions or other hostile acts by their would-be overlords.[17] And also by their enemies' plans for destroying all Jews[18] or at least abolishing Judaism and requiring Jews to the worship of their gods.[19]

IDOLATRY, APOSTASY AND SYNCRETISM

One final feature of Jewish life during the Seleucid/Maccabean years was religious syncretism, also known in biblical terms as apostasy (turning from the LORD) and idolatry.

Biblical stories, laws, and prophets had long insisted that Israel worship the LORD only, and reject all other gods or so-called gods. As will be seen, Nehemiah and Ezra vehemently opposed their contemporaries' inclination to worship their foreign wives' foreign gods during the Persian Period. Then during the Maccabean/Seleucid era, while living in the midst of other peoples and under domination of foreigners, Jews again were tempted to worship their neighbors' gods or

---

16. For example, similarities between Antiochus as represented in 1 Macc 1:20–64, and Dan 7:19–21, 8:11–13; 12:11. And their enemies' employment of elephants against Jews in both 1 Maccabees and 3 Maccabees.

17. See 1 and 2 Maccabees.

18. See Judith, Esther, 3 Maccabees.

19. See Daniel, and Bel and the Dragon.

idols.[20] And also, perhaps. the gods of the foreign nations or empires they might have believed had helped their enemies defeat them. Many writings composed during the last few centuries of the biblical period lament such apostasy, underscore the bogus nature of foreign gods or idols, and call for returning to the LORD. Extended critiques of idolatry are found in several biblical writings apparently dating from those years.

For example, the entire Letter of Jeremiah, is devoted to ridiculing belief in idols. As in the following excerpt:

> For just as one's dish is useless when it is broken, so are the gods of the heathen, when they have been set up in their temples. Their eyes are full of the dust raised by the feet of those who enter. . . . Bats, swallows, and birds light on their bodies and heads; and so do cats. From this you will know that they are not gods; so do not fear them.[21]

Other writings are aimed more at debunking the gods of the foreigners who ruled over them. For example, in the story of Bel and the Dragon, Daniel sets a trap for the priests of Bel, and demonstrates that they are engaged in fraud: "'Do not be deceived, O king, for this [image] is but clay inside and brass outside, and it never ate or drank anything'" (Bel v. 7).

Despite Hellenization, persecutions, apostasy, intrigues, and intermittent catastrophes, the Jewish people enjoyed some measure of autonomy during the Seleucid/Maccabean years. They were living on part of what had been their own country, and, at least for some of those years, during the Maccabean era, they were no longer mere sojourners on lands belonging

---

20. From the standpoint of the developed faith of Israel, these so-called gods were not gods at all, but merely man-made objects. See, e.g., Letter of Jeremiah and the story of Bel and the Dragon.

21. Letter of Jeremiah (or Baruch, chapter 6) 6:17–23. See also Wis chapters 13–15, Sir 30:19–20, and Bel. See also Isa 46:1–7.

to, or claimed by others. This era of at least quasi and struggling independence lasted for almost one hundred years.

UNDER ROMAN RULE

The Roman general, Pompey, had already annexed most of the region of Syria by 64/63 BCE. A few years later, the territory subsequently known as Palestine, was added to the domain of Rome. Once again, Jews had to live as sojourners on what once had been their own land.

Some Roman rulers were relatively benign, others harsh. During this period, the Temple was expanded and refurbished under the direction of Herod "the Great," an Edomite, appointed by the Romans as governor, who had been given the title of "King" by the Roman Senate.[22] But subsequent representatives of Roman authority cared little about Jewish sensibilities, and sometimes deliberately provoked them by actions contrary to Jewish custom or law.

Understandably, many Jews began to resent Roman rule, and in 66 CE, and led by the Zealot party, revolted. Soon Roman legions besieged Jerusalem. In 69/70 CE, Roman forces stormed into Jerusalem, destroyed most of the Temple, putting an end sacrificial offerings there, and banished Jews from Jerusalem.[23] This banishment was the final diaspora event in biblical times.[24] Banished Jews took up living in other parts of what was now the Roman world. There was no mass deportation, as before when their countries

22. Whatever his faults, which were many, Herod at least understood and was somewhat sensitive to Jewish religious concerns. But the fact that he was a foreigner, and perhaps worse, an Edomite, greatly diminished his popularity with his Jewish subjects.

23. A contingent of Jewish forces continued resistance at Masada, a mountain fortification, until 73 CE.

24. A final unsuccessful effort to gain independence from Rome broke out in 134–35 CE, under the leadership of Bar Cochba.

were over-fun by Assyria and Babylonia. Expelled Jews now might choose to live or sojourn wherever else they could go, at least to the extent that they were welcomed by other peoples and nations. This banishment constituted the final occasion when powerful enemies compelled large numbers of Israelites. Judahites or Jews to join the growing numbers already living abroad—in the diaspora—as sojourners.[25]

25. From the New Testament, we learn that many Jews already resided in various parts of the Roman world prior to 66 CE. The Apostle Paul, who is thought to have died ca. 64 CE, reportedly visited Jewish communities throughout the Roman world (Acts chapters 13–14). Josephus and Philo of Alexandria also lived abroad during this period.

Chapter Ten

Review and Preview

ISRAELITES, JUDAHITES, AND JEWS had lived as sojourners for well over half of the biblical period. that is, the nearly two thousand years between the time of Abraham, ca. 1800 BCE, and their final banishment ca. 70 CE. During most of those years they had sojourned in Egypt, Philistine and Hittite country, Canaan, Syria (Aram), Egypt (again), the Sinai Peninsula, Moab, Canaan (again), under Philistine rule (again), later as captives taken to Assyria, as exiles in Babylon, and finally—in what in earlier times had been their own country—under the rule of Persian, Greek, Egyptian (Ptolemaic), Syrian (Seleucid), and Roman empires. It is understandable that their modern descendants, after nearly two thousand years of living as diaspora, deeply longed to again live in that land and have it as their own.

Israelites, Judahites, and Jews had a variety of experiences as sojourners. Some, like Moses and David, sought refuge or asylum with other peoples in order to get away from prosecution or people seeking revenge.[1] Many more

1. Jacob, on his mother's advice, took refuge in Syria to avoid retribution by his twin brother, Esau, after Jacob had fraudulently obtained his father's

sojourned in other countries hoping to find food and places to live during periods of draught and famine.[2] Many more, sojourned *en route*, looking for lands where they might settle after leaving their former homes or homelands.[3] And most, perhaps, sojourned elsewhere involuntarily, after being deported or banished.[4]

A few features of biblical Israel's experience as sojourners might be mentioned here. Some of these may suggest beliefs, and moral insights and practices that could contribute to understanding and responding to critical situations in the modern world.

On various occasions, sojourners sought asylum with other peoples or countries as refugees and were well received.[5] But Israelite sojourners were not always welcomed when they ventured into new territories. Particularly if or when they tried to enter such territories by force of arms.[6]

---

blessing. Jacob then remained in Syria as a "guest worker," in order to obtain Rachel as his wife. Another example: the small group of Jews who sought refuge in Egypt following the catastrophic Babylonian conquest of rhe kingdom of Judah ca. 586 BCE (2 Kgs 25:22–26).

2. Abraham and Sarah, then Isaac and Rebekah in Egypt, and later all Israel in Egypt.

3. For instance, again, Abraham, Isaac, and their families after leaving Philistine country, Israel in the wilderness after leaving Egypt, and Israelite "tribes" moving (whether by war or gradual infiltration) into the land of Canaan during the time of Joshua and the Judges.

4. For instance, the final years of Israel's sojourn in Egypt, after their enslavement by the "new king who knew not Joseph"; the entire people of Israel (Northern Kingdom) who were deported to Assyria; Judahites living under Babylonian domination from 598 to 586 BCE; and the exiles who returned from Babylon whose descendants then were governed by Persia, Greek, Egyptian, Syrian, and finally Roman authorities.

5. Experience as refugees may have influenced the enactment of biblical laws establishing "cities of refuge" or sanctuary cities for persons seeking protection from vengeance while awaiting trial. As is well known, foreign immigrants seeking asylum prompt urgent concern in many parts of the modern world today.

6. Cf. relations between Native Americans and European settlers in

And on occasions when they were initially welcomed, they sometimes prospered so much that they aroused their neighbors' envy.[7] If they became "fruitful and multiplied" too much, they might be feared as a potential threat.[8] Sometimes host people were bothered by the sojourners' refusal to worship the national gods, and would try to require them to do so on pain of persecution or death.[9] Or for other reasons begin to exclude, persecute, deport or even try to annihilate them.[10]

On the other hand, sojourners might become too comfortable with their neighbors' ways, adopt some of their cultural practices, blend or mix their traditional beliefs (or theologies) with their neighbors' philosophies or ideologies, and conflate their traditional religious values with the religious or secular norms and mores of those around them.[11] These matters are, no doubt, worth fuller consideration elsewhere.

America.

7. A recurrent problem for latter-day European and American Jewish minorities whose levels of education and enterprise exceeded that of already established populations. And for many Asian and Asian-American residents in the United States.

8. E.g., the attitudes of white minorities in American states with substantial Black or Hispanic majorities. And particularly the fears of some Americans and many Europeans about the influx of, or "invasion" by large numbers of foreign immigrants.

9. Jews have long been subjected to periodic persecution by Christians for a variety of reasons, including their refusal to recognize Jesus as divine, or the idea that Jews were, and so all Jews forever are, responsible for Jesus execution (the "blood libel"). New Testament texts can be read either way, but show clearly that Jesus was crucified under Roman authority.

10. The great offense of people who are different from those who consider themselves the only people who count (or most closely resemble themselves), is that they are different. Bigotry of course has many sources and faces. Fascist and other nativist movements in Europe and the United States have at one time and another targeted Native Americans, Germans, Hispanics, African-Americans, Gypsies, Jews, Japanese, Chinese, and French people, Muslims, Near- and Mid-Easterners, and others. Especially as newly arrived or arriving immigrants.

11. See H. Richard Niebuhr's classic study of this phenomenon, *Christ and Culture*. And illustrations of contemporary versions described in Gushee,

The present study, however, examines only one such type of experience and related issues. This is, whether or how biblical Israelites' experience as sojourners in other communities and countries affected their attitudes and developing laws regarding the presence of foreign sojourners in their own midst. Were they welcomed? Only under particular circumstances? Did the Israelites' experience as sojourners in other lands give them greater awareness as to the feelings and needs of foreigners sojourning among them? To what extent were sojourners entitled to the same rights and privileges as native-born Israelites, Judahites, or Jews? And how did native-born Israelites or Jews regard other foreigners?

Throughout most of the biblical period, Israelites, Judahites, and Jews sojourned in lands belonging to others, or under the dominion of foreign peoples, nations, and empires. Except for relatively short periods of independence, they were longing for and trying to establish a country of their own, a land where they could live in peace with their neighbors, worship the LORD, follow the Law, and cherish the good gifts of creation.[12] Their long and often troubled experience as sojourners undoubtedly contributed to their latter day descendants' appreciation of again having and becoming again, a nation of their own. And, perhaps, appreciation of the experience, feelings, and needs of different racial, ethnic, and religious groups and individuals living within the borders of such a nation.

In the first part of this study, we trace in broad outlines the experiences of Israel and Israelites *as* sojourners. We

---

Following Jesus.

12. As expressed in many ways, among them aspiring to enjoy a "land flowing with milk and honey" and the prospect of living, at peace, each person "under his own vine and fig tree" (Exod 3:7–8; Mic 4:4). And see Amos 9:13–15, a vision of promise and hope that echoes the account of the good life experienced by the first man and woman in the Garden of Eden at the very beginning of the biblical story (Gen 2:4–24).

have seen that sojourning was at the core of Israel's history as a people. In this sense, they were a "nation of immigrants." They, themselves, were also a "nation of immigrants" in another way.

Since the days of Abram and Sarai, all the people of Israel were foreigners or descended from foreigners. How did they regard and relate to other foreigners, especially those sojourning with them? These matters are considered below, in Part Two.

Part Two

Sojourners

Biblical Attitudes and Laws
Regarding Foreign Immigrants

IN WHAT FOLLOWS, WE review biblical laws and traditions concerning the status of sojourners and other resident foreigners in biblical times. We begin Part Two with the classic story of the sojourner, Ruth, found in the biblical book which bears her name as its title.

After that, we examine stories and other traditions reflecting positive attitudes with respect to marriages between the people of Israel (and Judah) and those from other ethnic groups or nations. For instance, all the biblical "patriarchs"[1]

1. The term "patriarch" does not appear in the Hebrew Bible, but only in the later Septuagint, where it may reflect Greek conceptions of the relative status of men and women. See generally Beard, *Women & Power*. Such influence also may be evident in certain New Testament texts, e.g., John 2:1–5, 1 Cor 14:33–35, and 1 Tim 2:11–15. These texts insist on women's subordination to male authority. In the Hebrew text of Genesis, the so-called "patriarchs" are referred to simply as "fathers" and their wives as "mothers" of their respective progeny. See Hiers, *Women's Rights*), 3–8. The term "ancestors" more accurately represents the biblical understanding that both the "fathers" and "mothers" played major roles in the formation of what would become the people and nation of Israel, Judah, and the Jewish people.

married foreign women without exciting any adverse or prejudicial comment.

Later biblical figures and commentators, however, strongly opposed marriages with foreign women when such women then prompted their husbands to commit apostasy by worshiping their foreign gods. Some also objected to the people of "Israel" mixing themselves with foreigners, and producing progeny of mixed ancestry.

Yet many biblical traditions candidly acknowledge that the Jewish people and/or the people of Israel and Judah before them, were, themselves, people of mixed ancestry. All of their forefathers and foremothers were immigrants from other "tribes" or nations. They had experienced the hardships of sojourners in other peoples' lands. Thus they knew "the heart of a stranger" or sojourner. Therefore, many of their laws call on the people of Israel treat sojourners with justice and compassion; and to be careful to obey the laws of the LORD that provided sojourners the same legal protections and privileges as those enjoyed by native-born members of their communities.

Another fundamental reason for viewing and treating foreigners kindly, comes to expression in many other biblical traditions. Significant texts in both the Old Testament and the New recognized and demonstrated that all of humankind are related to one another biologically or genetically. And also by being, in common with other nations, the LORD's people, people for whom he cares, as he cares for all creation. This core belief and understanding is expressed both in what might otherwise seem dusty and dreary genealogies, and in a series of classic prophetic proclamations regarding the LORD's present and future intentions as to relations between and among Israel, other nations, all humankind, and all creation.

Chapter Eleven

Marriages and Relations with Foreigners

Positive Viewpoints

THE STORY OF RUTH, set in the land of Judah during the chaotic period of the Judges, shows that biblical laws were understood to protect and benefit foreign women. The story tells that Ruth, a sojourner from Moab, gleaned, that is, gathered food on fields belonging to a nearby land owner (and relative) named Boaz—all in accordance with laws providing for sojourners and other needy people to do so on the property of others.[1] Though a Moabite, Ruth also evidently enjoyed the benefits of two other customary or unwritten laws. One was the law or custom of levirate marriage, according to which a childless widow had the right to marry and be provided for by the brother or nearest kinsman of her deceased husband.[2] The story also touches on the right of

1. See below p. 64 n.3.

2. As to levirate marriage, see Hiers, *Women's Rights*, 42, 46–47, and same author, *Justice and Compassion*, 40–43, 199–202.

widows to inherit their deceased husbands' property, a right implicit in the narrative and other biblical traditions.

Ruth's story also illustrates the importance of foreign women in constituting the latter-day population of Israel and Judah. This Moabite sojourner is said to have been King David's great-grandmother, and thus also an ancestor of David's several descendants who for centuries occupied the throne of Judah and, briefly, that of Israel (Ruth 4:13–20; Matthew 1:5–17), and, many generations later, of Joseph, the "supposed" father of Jesus. (Luke 3:23–31.)[3]

OTHER MARRIAGES WITH FOREIGN WOMEN

Several other Old Testament narratives refer, without hesitation, to marriages with foreign women. Most notably, the marriages of all the so-called "patriarchs": Abraham, Isaac, and Jacob. Each of these "fathers of Israel" married Syrian (also known as Aramean) women: respectively Sarai (or Sarah),[4] Rebekah, and Rachel and Leah. Abraham also married Hagar, an Egyptian, who bore his first son, Ishmael.[5] Jacob's son, Judah, married a Canaanite woman, Shua, and later, his daughter-in-law, Tamar, also probably Canaanite, who bore him two sons, Perez and Zerah (Gen chapter 38). Perez is later identified as an ancestor of David (Ruth 4:18–22; Matt 1:3–36) and his descendants. Perez also was the presumptive forefather of the tribe or nation known in later biblical accounts as Perizzites. Another of Jacob's sons, Joseph, married Asenath, an Egyptian. Their children,

---

3. Cf. Matt 1:1–5, where Rahab—presumably the Canaanite harlot of Joshua 2:1–23—is named as another foremother of David's. And see below chapter 13.

4. Abraham, himself, may have been either Syrian or Chaldean.

5. See Hiers, *Women's Rights*, 4–5.

Ephraim and Manasseh, were the forefathers of the two "tribes" of Israel known by their names (Gen 41:45, 50–52). Moses likewise married foreign women. First Zipporah, the daughter of a Midianite priest with whom Moses took refuge as a sojourner after murdering an Egyptian (Exod 2:11–23). Later on, Moses also married a Cushite woman. As the story is told, Moses' brother, Aaron, and their sister, Miriam, objected to his marrying this, probably black, African woman. However, the LORD then chastises Aaron and Miriam for so objecting, and punishes Miriam by temporarily turning her color a leprous white (Num 12:1–15). The story seems to say that such marriages were, or should be considered unobjectionable. The Song of Solomon also reflects a positive attitude as to black women. Here the woman speaker declares, evidently with some pride, "I am black and beautiful" (1:5).[6] The Hebrew conjunction can be translated either as "and" or "but." In any case the reader could be expected to assume that "Solomon"[7] would have been happy to add this black and beautiful foreign woman to his assortment of foreign wives.

OTHER FOREIGN FRIENDS OF ISRAEL

Foreigners figure significantly in other Old Testament narratives. Among these, Moses' Midianite wife, Zipporah, who saves his life when, for no apparent reason, the LORD "sought to kill him" (Exod 4:24–26); Rahab, the Canaanite prostitute at Jericho, who hides the Israelite spies, enabling them to escape and report back to Joshua (Josh 2:1–23); and Jael, the Kenite woman who assassinates the leader of a hostile

---

6. Some more recent translations describe her as "very dark."

7. Whether or not the historical Solomon wrote the Song of Solomon, its lyrics are attributed to Solomon, and may be presumed to represent what he (or whoever the speaker was thought to have been) had said or would have said.

Canaanite army during the period of the Judges.[8] Also to be mentioned: Samson, who was infatuated with young Philistine women (Judg 14:1–20, 16:4–20), and Uriah the Hittite, one of David's faithful "mighty men" who had been married to Bathsheba until King David had him murdered and took her to be another of his own wives. (2 Sam 11:1–27). Ittai, the Gittite, a Philistine, was another of David's "mighty men" (2 Sam 18:2).

In these relatively early stories, marriage and friendly relations with foreigners seem to have been considered normal, or at least unremarkable. However, not all marriages and other connections with foreigners were viewed so favorably.

8. Judges 4:11–22; 5:24–27. Presumably Jael like her husband, Heber, also was a Kenite.

Chapter Twelve

Foreign Women, Foreign Gods

BIBLICAL TRADITIONS CLEARLY DISAPPROVE of marriage to foreign women in one set of circumstances. Namely, if or when these women were married to the kings of Israel or Judah, continued to worship their foreign deities, and persuaded their royal husbands and others to do likewise. Solomon's several foreign wives, and Ahab's Phoenician wife, Jezebel, are the most notable examples.

SOLOMON, HIS WIVES AND CONCUBINES

The Deuteronomic historian sets out in some detail the extent of Solomon's involvements with such women:

> Now King Solomon loved many foreign women: the daughter of Pharaoh, and Moabite, Ammonite, Edomite, Sidonian and Hittite women, from the nations concerning which the LORD had said to the people of Israel, "You shall not enter into marriage with them, neither shall they with you, for surely they will turn away your heart

after their gods."[1] Solomon clung to these in love. He had seven hundred wives, princesses, and three hundred concubines; and his wives turned away his heart. For when Solomon was old, his wives turned away his heart after other gods; and his heart was not wholly true to the LORD his God, . . . [2] For Solomon went after Ashtoreth the goddess of the Sidonians, and after Milcom, the abomination of the Ammonites. So Solomon did what was evil in the sight of the LORD and did not wholly follow the LORD as David his father had done. Then Solomon built a high place for Chemosh, the abomination of Moab, and for Molech, the abomination of the Ammonites, on the mountain east of Jerusalem. And so he did for all his foreign wives, who burned incense and sacrificed to their gods.[3]

It may be noteworthy that the historian/narrator expressed no concern about the presence of offspring from these mixed marriages, or of progeny resulting from Solomon's love affairs with his three hundred concubines, some if not all, also likely foreigners. Rather, the matter of concern was the worship of other gods.

The Deuteronomic writer[4] goes on to attribute the break-up of the (briefly) united kingdoms of Israel and Judah

1. Cf. Deut 7:1–16 (calling on the Israelites to utterly destroy all the people of the land of Canaan). Biblical scholars generally consider its extreme requirements a dramatic expression of the Deuteronomic historian's emphasis on the importance of remaining faithful to the LORD, and refusing to worship foreign gods, lest the LORD destroy them as had happened before when, as a result of their apostasy, the kingdoms of Israel and Judah were over-run by Assyria and Babylonia, respectively. The earlier version of the law set out in Exod 34:11–16 did not require the Israelites to kill off the inhabitants of the land they were invading.

2. The narrator/commentator did not object to Solomon's love affairs with the three hundred concubines. Notice that the commentator blames Solomon's *wives* for turning "away his heart after other gods," as if Solomon, himself, had no choice but to follow their lead.

3. 1 Kings 11:1–8.

4. Biblical scholars use the terms Deuteronomic writer, editor, or historian to characterize the hypothetical mid-sixth century, BCE individual,

to Solomon's apostasy, that is, his "going after" or worshiping these foreign gods. Doing so directly violated the first and fundamental commandment set out in all three versions of the "Ten Commandments": Exodus 20:3; 34:14, and Deut 5:7.

JEZEBEL, ASHERAH AND BAAL

Jezebel, the Phoenician wife of Ahab, King of Israel, was probably the most active and aggressive proponent of serving foreign deities. She promoted the worship of Asherah and Baal, both Canaanite gods. She not only fed "the four hundred and fifty prophets" of Baal and "the four hundred prophets of Asherah" at her royal table (1 Kings 18:19). She also ordered the execution of some of the LORD's prophets (1 Kings 18:13). All this was prelude to the famous, dramatic occasion when Elijah challenged and defeated the priests of Baal at Mt. Carmel (1 Kgs 18:20–40).

In both situations the problem was not that these kings had married foreign women. The problem was that these foreign wives had encouraged or induced their husbands—and apparently many other Judahites and Israelites—to worship their alien or foreign deities, and in the case of Jezebel, to sponsor their priests or prophets and authorize killing the LORD's prophets. As queen, Jezebel also acted the part of an unlimited monarch—unlimited by any acknowledgment of the LORD or his laws. Accordingly, she did not hesitate

---

individuals, or theological school, whose main concern was to emphasize the critical importance of worshiping the LORD and no other gods. His or their work is reflected in the books of Judges through 2 Kings. He or they reviewed and commented on the earlier history of Israel and Judah, attributing the catastrophes they had suffered to their violation of these and other commandments and requirements. See generally, Hiers, *Trinity Guide,* 17, 35, 51–2, 55–9, 72–4. In the present essay, as a convenience, we use masculine singular pronouns when referring to this individual or school, who may have been of either or both genders.

to arrange the murder of a nearby land owner who had refused to sell his ancestral property coveted by King Ahab, her husband. She then "gave" this land to her husband. (1 Kgs 21:1–16).

In time, the lure of foreign women affected many ordinary people as well. Marriages with such women became a matter of great concern to three figures or writers a few centuries later. Each held distinctive views, but all three objected to marriages with foreign women that resulted in people worshiping gods other than the LORD.

EZRA, NEHEMIAH, AND MALACHI

In addition to these commentaries on Solomon and Jezebel, two somewhat later biblical figures or writers, Ezra and Nehemiah, vividly expressed and exhibited negative and hostile attitudes regarding marriages with foreign women. Nehemiah appeared on the scene toward the middle of the Fifth Century BCE, as a local official or governor appointed by Persian authorities. (The former kingdom of Judah was now a province of the Persian Empire.) Nehemiah evidently felt strongly about this matter:

> "In those days . . . I saw the Jews who had married women of Ashdod, Ammon, and Moab; and half of their children spoke the languages of Ashdod, and they could not speak the language of Judah, but [only] the language of each people. And I contended with them and cursed them and beat some of them and pulled out their hair; and I made them take an oath in the name of God, saying, "You shall not give your daughters to their sons, or take their daughters for your sons or for yourselves. Did not Solomon king of Israel sin on account of such women? Among the many nations there was no king like him, and he was beloved by God, and God made him king over all Israel; nevertheless foreign women made

even him to sin. Shall we then listen to you and do all this great evil and act treacherously against our God by marrying foreign women?"[5]

Possibly Nehemiah had not considered the example of the "patriarchs" and Moses, who all had married foreign women.[6] Or perhaps he believed that foreign women would inevitably lead their husbands, sons, and daughters astray. However, unlike Ezra, who undertook to break up all such marriages, Nehemiah was content to make his Jewish male contemporaries forswear such marriages in the future (Neh 13:25).

Ezra was a major leader in the Jewish community around Jerusalem during the first half of the Fourth Century BCE, possibly as governor appointed by the Persian monarch Artaxerxes II. He was seriously dedicated to the tasks of promulgating and enforcing the Law or *Torah*. He was deeply concerned when he learned that many Jews, particularly priests and Levites, were marrying foreign women: notably, Canaanites, Hittites, Perizzites, Jebusites, Ammonites, Moabites, Egyptians, and Amorites. Doing so he believed would be sure to cause their husbands to worship their wives' foreign gods. Moreover, marrying these women meant that the "holy race" had "mixed itself" with these peoples (Ezra 9:1–2). On hearing about such misconduct, Ezra "rent" or tore his own clothes, pulled hair from his own head and beard, and "sat appalled" (Ezra 9:3). As the story is told, Ezra then presided over a great assembly of "Israelites"[7] and called

---

5. Nehemiah 13:23–27. Nehemiah objected to these marriages not only because the wives might (or would) induce their husbands to worship their foreign gods, but also because half the children of these marriages spoke foreign languages and could not speak Hebrew. In other words, he was prompted by both cultural and religious concerns.

6. See above chapter 11, and below chapter 13.

7. The Northern Kingdom, Israel, was over-run by Assyria in 722 BCE. The Southern Kingdom, Judah, survived until it was annexed by Babylonia,

on them to "put away" all their foreign wives and all the children of these mixed marriages (Ezra, chapter 10). What was to become of these divorced or "put away" women and children is not said. Like Nehemiah, Ezra seems not to have known (or remembered) that he and all his fellow Jews were descended from many foreign groups or nations and were, themselves, already a people of mixed ancestry.[8]

Ezra fervently wanted to protect "the holy race" and also "God's holy place" (Ezra 9:8), probably referring to Jerusalem, from becoming contaminated by marriages with foreign women and by the presence of their mixed offspring. Otherwise the LORD might punish them again[9] for failing to keep his commandments.

Near or shortly before the time of Nehemiah, the prophet Malachi also challenged his contemporaries' proclivity for marrying foreign women—at any rate, those who worshiped foreign gods (Mal 2:11-12). At the same time Malachi emphatically opposed divorce, and said nothing about "putting away" foreign wives or their children. Instead, he strongly urged husbands to be faithful to their wives (Mal 2:13-16). Even, it would seem, to their foreign wives.

Clearly these three—Malachi, Nehemiah and Ezra—believed that their fellow Jews should refrain from marrying foreign women, at any rate, those who worshiped foreign gods. Yet, as we have seen, in earlier centuries, marriage with foreign women was a matter of little or no concern.

---

marking the beginning of the exile, early in the Sixth Century, BCE. The exile ended when, in 539/38 BCE, the Persian emperor, Cyrus, gave the exiles permission to return to their former homeland. Many did so. But the nation Judah no longer existed. Around the time of Nehemiah, the people of the former Kingdom of Judah began to be called, and to call themselves "Jews," or, alternatively, "Israelites," or simply "Israel."

8. See next chapter, "A Nation of Immigrants."

9. See above chapter 9.

Chapter Thirteen

A Nation of Immigrants

THE IDEAL OF GENETIC or ethnic purity implicit in Ezra's and Nehemiah's words and deeds conflicts directly with attitudes and understandings expressed in earlier biblical narratives where people from many nations or ethnic groups contributed to the genetic make-up of those people identified in later biblical times as Jews.[1] Certain biblical texts expressly recognized or acknowledged the mixed ancestry of the people of Israel and Judah—and thus also of their descendants. One such text called for periodic recitation of the following ancient creedal formulation:

> A wandering Aramean was my father; and he went down into Egypt and sojourned there, few in number; and there he became a nation, great, mighty, and populous.[2]

This recitation was part of an annual covenant renewal ceremony which was to be carried out by all Israel. Here, the gathered people of Israel were to acknowledge their common

1. See above p. 57 n.7.
2. Deuteronomy 26:5.

history and their common descent from their Aramean (Syrian) forefather, Jacob.

THE "PATRIARCHS," THEIR FOREIGN WIVES AND THEIR FOREIGN PROGENY

Abraham was Jacob's grandfather. Abraham's wife, Sarah, was Syrian,[3] and Abraham, himself, either Syrian or Chaldean (Babylonian).[4] Their son, Isaac, would have been at least half Syrian. Isaac, himself, married a Syrian, Rebekah. Thus Isaac's son, Jacob, was at least three fourths Syrian. Jacob's twin brother, Esau, was said to be the forefather of the people of Edom.

Thus Edomites of succeeding generations would have been cousins (from first to n'th degree, however far "removed") of Jacob's descendants. According to the Book of Job, Job, a unique model of faith and righteousness, if not the most righteous person in the Bible, was an Edomite.[5] The biblical Book of Job was, of course, named for this Edomite, just as the Book of Ruth was named for that Moabite sojourner.

Two of Jacob's wives, Rachel and Leah, also were Syrians. Leah's sons were Reuben, Simeon, Levi, and Judah, while Rachel was the mother of Joseph and Benjamin. Joseph married Asenath, an Egyptian. This couple were the fore-parents of Ephraim and Manasseh, the forefathers of the "tribes" of

---

3. Genesis 11:28 –29 can be read to mean that both Abraham (Abram) and Sarah (Sarai) were Chaldean. However, Gen 25:19–20 indicates that she was Syrian (Aramean). This text says that Sarah was the sister of Laban, "the Aramean," and "daughter of Bethuel, the Aramean of Paddan-aram." See generally Steinberg, *Kinship and Marriage*.

4. Genesis 11:27–31; 15:7.

5. See Job 1:1–12 and 42:7–17.

Israel named for them. Thus the sons of Leah and Rachel would have been genetically, at least seven eighths Syrian.

As the ancestral story continues, Leah's son, Judah, becomes the forefather of the whole nation and people of Judah, people who, beginning sometime in the fifth century BCE, came to known as Jews. Thus according to the genealogies presented in the Book of Genesis, Judah, the father of the Jewish people was at least seven eighths Syrian. Both of Judah's wives apparently were Canaanites, so his (and their) children would have been one half Canaanite and the other half Syrian, unless, if Abraham had been Chaldean, they would have been half Canaanite, seven sixteenths Syrian, and the remaining sixteenth Chaldean.

EZEKIEL: A PEOPLE OF MIXED ANCESTRY

The Sixth Century prophet, Ezekiel, highlights this kind of mixed ancestry while chastising his contemporaries for their pride and misdeeds: "Your origin and your birth are of the land of the Canaanites; your father was an Amorite, and your mother a Hittite" (Ezek 16:2–3). And again: "Your mother was a Hittite and your father an Amorite. And your elder sister is Samaria, . . . and your younger sister . . . is Sodom" (Ezek 16:45–46).

Here Ezekiel challenges the people of Jerusalem, calling into question any pretensions they might entertain as to racial, cultural, or moral superiority. They are, he says, a people of mixed ancestry who, like their sisters Samaria and Sodom, "did abominable things." They were even worse than their sister Sodom, a people who were proud and haughty, indulging in a "surfeit of food, and prosperous ease," while failing to "aid the poor and needy" (Ezek 16:47–50). Providing such assistance was not merely an optional good deed or *mitzvah.*

Part Two: Sojourners

It was obligatory under a variety of laws intended to protect and provide for the "poor and needy," whose numbers regularly included sojourners. Such laws are considered in the following chapter.

Chapter Fourteen

Rights and Interests of Sojourners and Other Persons in Need

Typically, sojourners, whether refugees or other kinds of immigrants, would have had little or no property and few, if any, nearby kinsmen (or kinswomen)[1] to assist them in times of need. A surprising number of biblical laws deal with the rights and interests[2] of foreign sojourners.

---

1. The sojourner, Ruth, lived with Naomi, her mother-in-law.

2. Modern Western jurisprudence generally refers to "rights" which are grounded in constitutions or laws. Biblical tradition rarely uses "rights" language. Instead, biblical laws refer to the responsibilities of persons in the community who have wealth or power. Laws such as those considered here emphasize their obligation to protect and provide for the interests or welfare of sojourners and other poor or needy persons. See generally, Patrick, *Old Testament Law*, and Hiers, "Biblical Social Welfare Legislation," 40–96.

EQUAL PROTECTION OF THE LAWS

Some laws expressly state that *all biblical laws* were meant to apply equally to Israelites and to sojourners,[3] who thereby, it might be said, were entitled to what in modern American jurisprudence is called "the equal protection of the laws." For instance, the following:

> The stranger who sojourns with you shall be to you as the native among you, and you shall love him as yourself; for you were strangers in the land of Egypt. I am the LORD your God.[4]

> You shall have one law for the sojourner and for the native; for I am the LORD your God.[5]

> For the assembly, there shall be one statute for you and for the stranger who sojourns with you, a perpetual statute throughout your generations; as you are, so shall the sojourner be before the LORD. One law and one ordinance shall be for you and for the stranger who sojourns with you. [6]

Like everyone else in the community, sojourners were entitled to rest on the Sabbath day. This provision is included in both commonly cited versions of the "Ten Commandments" (Exod 20:8–10, and Deut 5:12–14), though

3. The story of Ruth, considered above, illustrates such equal application with regard to two kinds of law: those as to gleaning, and the customary (if not yet written) law governing widows' right to marry their deceased husbands' next of kin. It also provides evidence that the customary or unwritten law of intestate succession meant that foreign widows could inherit their deceased husbands' property. See above chapter 11. The story of Ruth shows that these laws were understood to apply to foreign sojourners.

4. Leviticus 19:34.

5. Leviticus 24:22. It has been suggested that Lev 25:47–54 means that sojourners could be made permanent slaves. That meaning is not apparent in this text.

6. Numbers 15:15–16. See also Num 15:29–51. But see Num 15:14. This and similar laws may also imply that *gerim* were obliged to obey all laws in the same way as native-born members of the community.

generally omitted from inscriptions purporting to represent the "Ten Commandments" seen on courthouse squares and other public and religious settings in the United States. As read, the Sabbath law was more of a gift than a task. It meant that not only "native" Israelites, but also sojourners, servants, slaves, and even farm animals were to be free to rest on this day, every week, and every year. It seems likely that this law was inspired by Israel's experience as slaves in the land of Egypt.[7]

AFFIRMATIVE ACTION

Gerim or sojourners were to be assisted through a series of arrangements for meeting their need for food. One type of law obligated property owners to allow sojourners—along with other classes of vulnerable or needy persons—to "glean" or gather grain, olives, and fruit from their fields, vineyards and orchards. For instance, as commanded in Deut 24:19–22:

> When you reap your harvest in your field, and have forgotten a sheaf in the field, you shall not go back to get it; it shall be for the sojourner, the fatherless, and the widow: that the LORD your God may bless you in all the work of your hands. When you beat your olive trees, you shall not go over the boughs again; it shall be for the sojourner, the fatherless, and the widow. When you gather the grapes of your vineyard, you shall not glean it afterward; it shall be for the sojourner, the fatherless, and the widow. You shall remember that you were a slave in the land of Egypt; therefore I command you to do this.[8]

7. See also Deut 5:6,15: "You shall remember that you were a servant in the land of Egypt, and the LORD your God brought you out thence . . ."

8. Again, we see that Israel's experience as "a slave" in Egypt was a motive for the remarkable concern for the welfare of slaves expressed in biblical law. See also, Deut 24:17–18. See Patrick, *Old Testament Law*, 90, 168, and Hiers, *Justice and Compassion*, 203–9.

Leviticus 19:9–10 and 23:22 set out similar welfare laws.

In addition, sojourners were entitled to share the food brought in for celebrating the periodic agricultural festivals. For instance, as provided in Deut 16:13–14:

> You shall keep the feast of booths seven days, when you make your ingathering from your threshing floor and your wine press; you shall rejoice in your feast, you and your son and your daughter, your manservant and your maidservant, the Levite, the sojourner, the fatherless, and the widow who are within your towns.

Similar texts include Deut 6:9–12 (feast of weeks) and 26:1–11 (first fruits).

In order to provide food year-round for sojourners and others in need, another biblical law called for establishing permanent local food banks.

> At the end of every three years you shall bring forth all the tithe of your produce in the same year, and lay it up within your towns, and the Levite, because he has no portion or inheritance with you, and the sojourner, the fatherless, and the widow, who are within your towns, shall come and eat and be filled, that the LORD your God may bless you in all the work of your hands that you do.[9]

A related law required each property owner who should have brought in his or her third year tithes, to swear before the LORD, saying that he/she had really done so and had given it to "the Levite, the sojourner, the fatherless, and the widow, according to all thy commandment which thou hast commanded me" (Deut 26:12–15). These laws roughly parallel (or provide precedent for) modern American legislation establishing such government sponsored programs as food

---

9. Deuteronomy 14:28–29. It might be noted that the tithe was meant to help provides for those in the community who were in need, not as an obligation to contribute to religious institutions or their personnel.

stamps and Aid to Families with Dependent Children, as well as other publicly and privately sponsored services such as local food pantries or food banks.[10]

LAWS AGAINST DISCRIMINATION

Some laws explicitly prohibited oppressing or discriminating against sojourners or treating them as if they were non- or second-class citizens. For example:

> You shall not oppress a stranger; you know the heart of a stranger, for you were strangers in the land of Egypt.[11]

> When a stranger sojourns with you in your land, you shall not do him wrong. The stranger who sojourns with you shall be to you as the native among you, and you shall love him as yourself; for you were strangers in the land of Egypt: I am the LORD your God.[12]

> You shall not pervert the justice due to the sojourner or to the fatherless, or take a widow's garment in pledge; but you shall remember that you were a slave in Egypt and the LORD your God redeemed you from there; therefor I command you to do this.[13]

These laws regarding sojourners did not distinguish between men and women, or between adults and children, but clearly were meant to apply to all resident aliens or *gerim*. Nor did they distinguish between political and economic refugees. Nor did they include any provision for inquiring as to how or why these sojourners were there, or their country of origin, their marital status, their means of support, what

---

10. And such international support agencies such as Amnesty International, the Red Cross, the International Committee on Refugees, and UNHCR, the United Nations Refugee Agency. See Hiers, *Justice and Compassion* 165–216.

11. Exodus 23:9.

12. Leviticus 19:33–34.

13. Deuteronomy 24:17–18.

skills they had to contribute, whether they had relatives who could vouch for them, or whether they were likely to become a public charge. Rather, these laws are entirely consistent with core biblical understandings as to the basis for human existence, and for every other thing that exists in all creation. And consistent with the understanding that the LORD's people were expected to conduct themselves accordingly, whether individually or as a nation.

Moreover, these understandings and obligations rest upon recognition that all human beings share a common ancestry and common history, and are, therefore, related to one another, however distantly. Modern genetic theories to some extent parallel this biblical faith understanding.

Chapter Fifteen

Foreigners, and Native-Born

All Are Related and All Belong to the LORD

THE LAWS PROTECTING THE rights and interests of sojourners are entirely congruent with, and give concrete expression
to core biblical beliefs, understandings, and affirmations ac-
knowledging the LORD as the Creator of all humankind—
humankind that God had deemed not only good, but, like
everything else he had made, "very good" (Gen 1:24–31).
This and another Genesis text declare three times that God
created man, both male and female, "in his own image" (Gen
1:26–27; 5:1–2). All human beings.[1]

---

1. What may have been meant originally by the expression "image of God"
has been discussed at length by biblical scholars and theologians. Whatever
that meaning may have been, it was apparently understood that all humans,
both male and female were created equally in that same image. See Gushee,
Sacredness of Human Life, 41–46, 390–92.

DESCENDED FROM THE PRIMORDIAL PAIRS: ADAM AND EVE, NOAH ET UX.

The members of the first primordial pair are identified as the forefather and foremother of human beings of all races, nationalities, cultures, places, and times. Initially all peoples even spoke the same language and lived together in one place (Genesis chapter 11).[2]

The biblical flood story (Gen 5:32—9:19) traces human origins to another primordial pair: Noah and his wife. Here it is said that the flood destroyed "all flesh that moved upon he earth," *except for* Noah and his wife, their three sons and their wives; and pairs of every other kind of living thing, for the purpose of keeping them alive so "that they may breed abundantly upon the earth, and be fruitful and multiply upon the earth" (Gen 6:11—8:19).[3] All later-born human beings were, the story says, descended from the sons of Noah and their wives.[4]

It may be mentioned, in connection with the matter of biblical attitudes toward foreigners, that some years ago, a distorted version of this story, Gen 9:20–27, was often evoked

2. It need not be assumed that these stories about early humankind have meaning only if understood as literal or actual history. Instead, they can be understood as rather profound ways of trying to answer fundamental existential questions. Questions such as why man and woman experience a strong desire to be together; why people do not live forever; whether human life has meaning and value; or why people recognize kinship bonds with others, yet are separated from one another, living in different lands and nations, and even speaking different languages.

3. It is noteworthy that "every living creature of all flesh that was upon the earth" was told to be "fruitful and multiply upon the earth" after the flood (Gen. 8:17; 9:15-16). Former U.S. Interior Secretary, Bruce Babbitt once characterized this episode as the world's first endangered species act. See Isenberg, "Continue Noah's Legacy," F5. And see, Gushee, *Sacredness of Human Life*, 401–04.

4. Genrsis chapters 8–10. See Gen 9:19: "These were the sons of Noah, and from these the whole earth was peopled."

by people who wished to justify racially based slavery and segregation. In effect, it was said that here God cursed one of these sons, Ham (assumed to have been a black African), and declared that he and his descendants were to be slaves to his brothers (assumed to have been white or Caucasian) and their descendants. Closer reading of the text, however, reveals that it was not God, but Noah, emerging from a drunken stupor, who did the cursing, and that the person cursed was not Ham, but Canaan. In later years, as mentioned in several texts already considered, Israelites did not hesitate to marry Canaanites. Although later scattered abroad over the face of the earth, all human beings were understood to be related to one another through their common ancestors: first from Adam and his wife, and then Noah and his wife. So likewise Paul in his Areopagite sermon: "And (God) made from one every nation of men to live on all the face of the earth . . ." (Acts 17:26). One might amend this to read "from one pair" rather than just "one." Perhaps this is what Paul meant to say.

OTHER NATIONS, FAMILY RELATIONS

Biological connections were not then understood in terms of shared or common DNA. However, the series of narratives and genealogies included in the Book of Genesis, along with statements in other biblical texts, characterize many neighboring nations or peoples as kin, that is, related to the people of Israel or Judah as brother or sister, half-brother, father and son, mother and son, and cousin or nephew. Such nations or peoples as Amorites, Ishmaelites, Canaanites, Hittites, Egyptians, Edomites, Syrians, Moabites, Perizzites, Ammonites, Sodomites, and (in later times, after Judah and Israel had parted company) Samaritans.[5] This faith-understanding—

5. See Gaster, "Samaritans," 19 *Encyclopedia Britannica* 918–19; and, same author, "Samaritans," 4 *Interpreter's Dictionary.*180–97.

that all peoples are the LORD's people, and part of a larger community of humankind—forms the backdrop for the entire biblical story, law, wisdom, and prophetic tradition. [6]

Many other biblical texts testify to the core belief and understanding that from the beginning God affirmed, and continued to affirm the well-being of all nations or peoples. And the belief that Israel was called on to act in such ways as to put this belief and understanding into effect through its relations with other nations. Relations with other nations is a central theme in most of the prophetic books of the Bible.

6. See H. Richard Niebuhr, *Radical Monotheism* 24–63 and 100–26, and Reinhold Niebuhr, *Children of Light* 133–89.

Chapter Sixteen

The Prophets, Israel, and Foreign Nations

NOTWITHSTANDING THE BONDS OF kinship remembered and celebrated in these narratives and traditions, many Old Testament texts do not view foreign nations with favor. In particular, many of the prophets declared that some or all such nations were or soon would be subject to the LORD's adverse judgement in the form of major catastrophes. These "oracles against foreign nations" proclaimed that certain foreign nations were to be punished in one way and another for their offenses against the LORD and his people.[1]

These nations would experience such judgment *not* because they were foreign, but rather, because of their misdeeds. Likewise, the people of Israel and their nations would be judged, typically through devastation at the hands of foreign nations, for their offenses against the LORD and his covenant with them. Notable examples include Jeremiah 2:1—5:3, Hosea 8:1–14, Amos 2:4–8, 4:6–12; and Isaiah 9:8—10:6. Moreover the LORD would also punish foreign

---

1. For example: Jer 25:15–38, Ezek 28:1–23, and the entire Book of Nahum.

nations for atrocities they had committed against the people of other nations (Jer 46:1–26; Amos 1:6—2:3).[2]

Nevertheless, the prophets did not condemn Israel and other nations to perpetual suffering or destruction. Most of the prophets offered their fellow Israelites and Judahites the certain hope that the LORD would eventually restore their fortunes. Other nations also remain the LORD's people, and, in time, he would again gather them into one fold, where they would be completely at peace with Israel and Judah and each other. This promise and hope for the future finds expression in a number of prophetic texts. The classic passage in this connection is Isa 49:6:

> It is too light a thing that you should be my servant to raise up the tribes of Jacob and restore the preserved of Israel; I will give you as a light to the nations, that my salvation may reach to the end of the earth.[3]

This mission or task is illustrated in the somewhat ironic story about the prophet Jonah.

The Book of Jonah, appears to have been written as a parable. The story tells how the LORD ordered Jonah to go and preach to Nineveh, thwarted his attempts to avoid doing so, and finally brought him to this city, which was the capitol of Assyria, an ancient enemy of Israel, in order to call its people to repentance. Following his grueling experiences at sea en route, Jonah then went about Nineveh eagerly proclaiming its impending doom. But to his profound consternation and chagrin, in response to his angry and unpromising message, the people[4] of Nineveh repented and were spared the destruction Jonah persisted in hoping to see. Responding to Jonah's

---

2. See e.g. Amos 1:9 "For three transgressions of Tyre and for four, I will not revoke the punishment, because they delivered up a whole people to Edom, and did not remember the covenant of brotherhood."

3. Thus also Isa 42:1–4; and see Tob 14:6–7.

4. And also cattle. Jon 3:6–9.

exasperated and vehement complaints, the LORD, answered: "Should not I pity Nineveh, that great city, in which there are more than a hundred and twenty thousand [little children], and also much cattle?" (Jon 4:31). It seems that the LORD cared about these foreigners (and their cattle), not just about the people of Israel and Judah.[5]

Another text in Isaiah looks forward to a future time of fulfillment when all the inhabitants of the world would again live together in peace and harmony:

> In that day Israel will be the third with Egypt and Assyria, a blessing in the midst of the earth, whom the LORD of hosts has blessed, saying, "Blessed be Egypt my people, and Assyria the work of my hands, and Israel my heritage."[6]

Two other famous prophetic texts likewise affirm in glowing poetic language the biblical hope and promise that the time would come when all people, indeed, all creation, would be at peace and "know the LORD." One of these is the "floating oracle," so called because it is found in two different

---

5. Those who take the story of Jonah literally as history or as prophecy to be fulfilled in later times, misread the story and miss its point. See, for instance, *Tobit* 14:4, 8. Like New Testament parables, the story of Jonah ends with a question, and leaves it up to the hearer or reader to grasp its message. The climax and key to the whole story, of course, is the question put to Jonah in the last sentence of the book. The narrator does not say whether Jonah, himself, ever understood—or was willing to accept—its meaning. See Hiers, *Trinity Guide*, 114–16.

6. Isaiah 19:24. These texts recall the LORD's promise to Abraham that he (and by implication, his descendants) would be a blessing to all the families of the earth Gen 12:1–3. The LORD makes a similar promise to Jacob (Gen. 28:13–14). The story about Joseph's establishing a major food storage program in Egypt ahead of seven years of world-wide famine, could be seen as a partial fulfilment of this promise. At the end of the story, Joseph explains to his brothers: "As for you, you meant evil against me; but God meant it for good, to bring it about that many people should be kept alive, as they are today." Gen 50:20. According to Gen 41:57, "*all the earth* came to Egypt to Joseph to buy grain, because the famine was severe over all the earth." Emphasis added.

prophetic writings: Micah 4:1–4, and Isaiah 2:2–4. Micah's version reads as follows:

> It shall come to pass in the latter days
>> that the mountain of the house of the LORD
> shall be established as the highest of the mountains,
>> and shall be raised up above the highest hills;
> and peoples shall flow to it,
>> and many nations shall come and say:
> "Come, let us go up to the mountain of the LORD,
>> to the house of the God of Jacob,
> that he may teach us his ways
>> and we may walk in his paths."[7]
> For out of Zion shall go forth the law,
>> and the word of the LORD from Jerusalem.
> He shall judge between many peoples,
>> and shall decide for strong nations afar off;
> and they shall beat their swords into ploughshares,
>> and their spears into pruning hooks;
> Nation shall not lift up sword against nation,
>> neither shall they learn war any more;
> but they shall sit every man under his own vine
>> and under his fig tree, and none shall make them afraid;
> for the mouth of the LORD of hosts has spoken.

Isaiah records one more vision of the future: where all creation will be at peace and the whole earth filled with "the knowledge of the LORD":

> The wolf shall dwell with the lamb,
>> and the leopard shall lie down with the kid,
> and the calf and the lion and the fatlng together,
>> and a little child shall lead them.
> The cow and the bear shall feed;
>> their young shall lie down together;
>> and the lion shall eat straw like the ox.
> The sucking child shall play over the hole of the asp,
>> and the weaned child shall put his hand on the adder's den.

7. Cf. Zech 14:16–19, where this prophet says that all the families and nations of the earth will come to Jerusalem to worship and keep the feast of booths—or else be punished for failing to do so.

They shall not hurt or destroy in all my holy mountain,[8]
  for the earth shall be full of the knowledge of the LORD,[9]
  as the waters cover the sea.

Similarly, the prophet Hosea: "And I will make for you a covenant on that day with the beasts of the field, the birds of the air, and the creeping things of the ground, and I will abolish the bow, the sword, and war from the land; and I will make you lie down in safety." [10]

NEW TESTAMENT HOPES AND PROMISES AS TO RELATIONS WITH OTHER PEOPLES AND NATIONS

Several New Testament texts reflect similar hopes. For instance, Jesus responds—after initial hesitation—to a Syrian-Phoenician (or Canaanite) mother's plea for help (Mark 7:24–30; Matt 15:21–28). And he tells a parable in which a Samaritan provides urgent care for an injured man, while two self-important religious functionaries pass by on the other side of the road (Luke 10:29–37). Also his promise that "[M]en will come from east and west, and from north and south, and sit at table in the kingdom of God" (Luke 13:29). The risen Jesus sends his followers out into the world to baptize and teach "all nations" all that he had commanded them (Matt 28:19–20).[11] And Paul, himself, undertook to preach the gospel to the Gentiles, meaning all other nations

---

8. Thus also Isa 65:25.

9. Isaiah 11:6–9. Cf. Jer 31:34: "And no longer shall each man teach his neighbor and each his brother, saying 'Know the LORD,' for they shall all know me, from the least of them to the greatest, says the LORD." See also 1 Cor 13:12: "Now I know in part; then I shall know fully, even as I have been known."

10 Hosea 2:18.

11. See also Matt 12:17–22, quoting Isaiah 42:1–4, and, Acts 8:26–39, the story about the conversion and baptism of an Ethiopian.

or peoples.[12] The mission to Gentiles or other nations is the central theme in the Book of Acts.[13]

In short, biblical law and tradition in a variety of ways give expression to the core biblical belief and understanding that all human beings and nations, whatever their differences, are the LORD's people and fully human. And can look forward to being together enjoying peace and well-being with each other and with all creation. Even sojourners—whether called foreigners, refugees, asylum-seekers, strangers, immigrants, or resident aliens—no matter what their ages, genders, or nations of origin.

Since biblical times, hundreds of millions of people from countless countries—willingly or unwillingly—have become sojourners in other peoples' lands. Like many other nations both ancient and modern, the United States of America was founded by sojourners. And sojourners have been coming from all the earth ever since.

---

12. Galatians 1:16; 2:1–10; Eph 3:4–8.

13. See Hiers, *Trinity Guide*, 206–9.

Chapter Seventeen

Sojourners Then, and Sojourners Now

Concluding Reflections

THIS ESSAY IS INTENDED to identify and high-light the re-markable number of biblical laws and traditions regarding the status of sojourners or foreign immigrants. And so we have tried to let the texts speak for themselves, with minimal commentary.[1] We leave it to others to consider practical implications of these laws and traditions for understanding and dealing with the often complex problems and policies regarding refugees, immigrants, and other kinds of sojourners in the modern world.[2] We offer here just a few observations and comments by others.

1. Some excellent studies on biblical law, ethics, and social policy are cited in the bibliography.

2. For instance, former President Jimmy Carter, commenting on this complexity, observed: "In the final analysis, the different parts of the Middle East have their own viewpoints, their own grievances, their own goals and aspirations. But it is Israel that remains the key, the tiny vortex around which swirl the winds of hatred, intolerance, and bloodshed. The indomitable people of Israel are still attempting to define their future, the basic character of their nation,

Part Two: Sojourners

Newly discovered DNA patterns now make it possible to trace genetic connections between and among many, if not most living and deceased human beings going back many generations. It is not uncommon to find that one's existence in this life is indebted to previously unknown and often ancient ancestors who lived on two or more different continents, in ten or more ancient and modern nations, and drawn from multiple racial and ethnic groups, including Neanderthals, *all of whose other descendants are now, necessarily, one's own and each other's relatives.*

Even before DNA discoveries, many people were aware of their mixed ancestry. The late Will Rogers once quipped that when his ancestors came over to America in the Seventeenth Century, and were getting off the boat, they were greeted by his ancestors—the ones who were Indians[3]—the original (at least earliest known) Native Americans—whose residence in the Americas preceded the arrival of all us more recent sojourners by several thousand years. As the late John F. Kennedy captioned his book on immigration to America, we are a "Nation of Immigrants,"[4] He might as well have entitled his book, "A Nation of Sojourners."

Whether or not such biblical texts as those considered in this book contributed directly or indirectly to Eighteenth Century "Enlightenment" beliefs and assertions to the effect that all human beings are equally important or valuable, is a

---

its geographical boundaries, and conditions under which the legitimate rights of the Palestinians can be honored and an accommodation forged with their neighbors. These internal decisions will have to be made in consultation with Arabs who are basically antagonistic—perhaps as difficult a political prospect as history has ever seen." Carter, *Palestine Peace*, 17–18.

3. The present writer's father, Glen S. Hiers, an admirer of Rogers, shared this story many years ago.

4. Kennedy, *Nation of Immigrants*, describing the history of immigration to America, some of the hardships and barriers immigrants encountered and overcame, and their contributions to this Country.

question beyond the scope of this study.[5] Those who drafted the *Declaration of Independence* believed it to be a "self-evident truth" that "all men are created equal," a proposition characterized by the late H. Richard Niebuhr as "the democratic dogma of equality."[6]

This belief or dogma is the foundation stone of American democracy, and came to be embodied in the *United States Constitution*, notably in the Fifth and Fourteenth Amendments.[7] Like the many biblical laws that apply in their terms to natives and sojourners alike, the language of the Fourteenth Amendment is inclusive. It prohibits states from denying "*any person* of life, liberty, or property, without due process of law," [or denying] "*any person* within its jurisdiction the equal protection of the laws."[8] The Fourteenth Amendment applies to actions by state and local governments, the Fifth

---

5. See Katsh, *Biblical Heritage of American Democracy*. Also Welch, "Bible in American Law" in Friedman, *Encyclopedia*, 124–31. Also same author, "Biblical Law in America." It may be mentioned here that there are many echoes of, or parallels between biblical law and modern Anglo-American jurisprudence. See Hiers, "Ancient Laws," 173–96), and same author, *Justice and Compassion*. Most of the American founding "fathers" (and mothers) very likely were familiar with the Bible and biblical norms and laws. It is commonly assumed that modern democratic beliefs and institutions derive from classical (Greek and Roman) customs and laws. These, however, had little to say about human rights, gender equality, or social welfare. See Beard, *Women & Power*, and same author, *SPQR*, 435–73.

6. H. Richard Niebuhr, *Radical Monotheism*, 73–77. Niebuhr pointed out that belief in human equality is rooted in faith, and represents an affirmation of the equal worth or value of human beings, rather than a statement of fact grounded on empirical evidence or rational argument. Such faith is consistent with, if not derived from, the kinds of biblical affirmations, hopes, and laws considered in this essay. As has been pointed out by many modern moral philosophers and critics, it is difficult if not impossible to derive normative evaluations from data or reason alone. See, e.g., Lewis, *Abolition of Man*, 67–91.

7. And implicitly in the Thirteenth and Fifteenth Amendments, which were intended to provide for just and equal rights for descendants of involuntary sojourners in this Country, namely, slaves brought here from Africa.

8. Article xiv, Section 1, emphasis added.

Amendment to actions by the Federal government. The U.S. Supreme Court has long held that the right to equal protection is inherent in the Fifth Amendment's Due Process Clause, which reads, in relevant part: "[N]or shall *any person* . . . be deprived of his life, liberty, or property, without due process of law" (emphasis added).[9] It appears that the expression "any person" in both Amendments should include sojourners or immigrants of any description, whatever their race, religion, color, gender, age, national origin, or any other distinctive, or purportedly significant differences there might be.[10]

The principle of "equal protection" has been incorporated into various civil rights laws such as Title VII of the Civil Rights Act of 1964 and as subsequently amended.[11] Title VII specifically prohibits employment discrimination based on race, color, religion, sex, or national origin. Discrimination against latter-day sojourners, whether characterized as immigrants, refugees or foreigners of any descriptions, would appear to constitute discrimination under such laws.

Like the visions of Israel's role or mission in the world as a "light for the nations" or a "blessing in the midst of the earth," many Americans have considered it important for our Country to serve as a model of democracy and a beacon of hope for other nations and peoples seeking to achieve peace, prosperity, justice, and freedom of the kind we enjoy in America. So believed the famous ex-slave and devoted

---

9. Cf. the text of the "Pledge of Allegiance": "I pledge allegiance to the flag of the United States of America, and to the Republic for which it stands: one Nation indivisible (or under God), with liberty and justice *for all.*" Emphasis added.

10. This reading of these Amendments has been challenged in federal courts by some who prefer to believe this constitutional language should apply only to persons who are already citizens.

11. Also known as the Equal Employment Opportunity Act, 42 U.S.C. sect. 2000e *et seq.*

patriot, Frederick Douglass. David W. Blight recently described Douglass's position in this regard:

> "In his 'Composite Nationality speech,' Douglass explained that nationhood 'implies a willing surrender and subjection of individual aims and ends, often narrow and selfish, to the broader and better ones that arise out of a society as a whole. It is both a sign and a result of civilization.' And a nation requires a story that draws its constituent parts into a whole. The post- (Civil) war United States served as a beacon—'the perfect national illustration of the unity and dignity of the human family.'"[12]

Despite recurrent (and current) nativist and xenophobic moments and movements,[13] welcoming immigrants has been an important part of American ideals and values since the early days of colonial America.

Such welcoming is proclaimed in the words of Emma Lazarus's poem inscribed at the base of the Statue of Liberty in New York Harbor: "Give me your tired, your poor, your huddled masses yearning to breathe free . . ."[14] Ms. Liberty and these words inscribed below her statue were, obviously, intended to invite and welcome sojourners, whether refugees or other kinds of immigrants, to these shores so that they might take part in the life of this great Nation. The only

---

12. Blight, "Frederick Douglass's Vision," 5. Quoted by permission of *The Atlantic.*

13. Some of which involved genocide, and continue to take the form of oppressive laws, harassment, and terrorist acts against racial and ethnic minorities. In early colonial times, immigrants from Europe sometimes thought of themselves as "Israelites" authorized to drive out or destroy native Americans who were viewed as "Canaanites." The ways Native Americans and immigrant populations (notably Hispanic, Chinese, Japanese, German, Mormon, Catholic, Jewish, and Muslim) have been treated in this Country are subjects commonly omitted from school-book histories of the United States.

14. Quoted in Kennedy, *Nation of Immigrants,* 77. The present writer recalls listening to a musical rendition of this text being sung with apparent pride and enthusiasm at the 1952 Republican National Convention in Philadelphia.

nation in the world whose citizens regularly pledge their commitment to "liberty and justice for all."

Or, as President George Washington put the matter:

> The bosom of America is open to receive not only the opulent and respectable stranger, but the oppressed and persecuted of all nations and religions, whom we shall welcome to a participation of all our rights and privileges, if by decency and propriety of conduct they appear to merit the enjoyment.[15]

Those who find the Bible a source of wisdom and guidance might well agree that this is how it should be.

15. Quoted in Kennedy, *Nation of Immigrants*, 83.

Postscript[1]

HUMAN BEINGS ARE CAPABLE of treating their fellowmen with both cruelty and kindness in all their relations. . . . Yet the chief source of man's inhumanity to man seems to be the tribal limits of his sense of obligation to other men.

At this very moment in history, cruelties aggravated by human tribalism occupy the news and preoccupy our minds. America, which has prided itself on being the "melting pot" of many ethnic groups, is, with great difficulty, trying to erase the last remnant of slavery a century after the Civil War. All over the world, there are struggles where new nations are being born, inevitably accompanied by these same inhumanities. . . .

. . . Any distinguishing mark between the "we group," in which mutual responsibilities are acknowledged, and a "they group," who are [seen as] outside the pale of humanity, may serve the tribal character of human nature. The distinguishing marks of tribalism may consist of common racial origins, or language, or religion and or class.[2]

1. Reinhold Niebuhr, *Man's Nature*, 84, 85. It should be noted that when Niebuhr was writing, terms such as "man," "mankind," and "humankind" were commonly understood as gender inclusive.

2. Niebuhr's critique of "tribalism" is paralleled to some extent by his brother H. Richard's description of "henotheism" in *Radical Monotheism*, 64–73 and 100–26, and Erich Fromm's portrayal of "social narcissism" in *The Heart of Man*, 62–94.

Bibliography

Beard, Mary, *Women & Power: A Manifesto.* London: Liveright / W.W. Norton, 2017.

———. *SPQR: A History of Ancient Rome.* London: Liveright, 2015.

Bellah, Robert et al., *Habits of the Heart: Individualism and Commitment in American Life.* Berkeley and Los Angeles: University of California Press, 1985.

Blight David W., "Frederick Douglass's Vision for a Reborn America." In the *Atlantic Monthly* Magazine, December 2019, http//www.the atlantic.com/magazine/Frederick-douglass-david-blight-america/600802/

Boecker, Hans Jochen, *Law and the Administration of Justice in the Old Testament and the Ancient Near East.* Translated by Jeremy Moiser. Minneapolis: Augsburg, 1980.

Brin, Gershon, *Studies in Biblical Law: From the Hebrew Bible to the Dead Sea Scrolls.* Translated from the Hebrew by Jonathan Chipman. Sheffield: Sheffield Academic, 1994.

Burnside, Jonathan, *God, Justice, and Society: Aspects of Law and Legality in the Bible.* Oxford University Press, 2011.

Burrows, Millar, *An Outline of Biblical Theology.* Philadelphia: Westminster, 1946.

———. *Palestine Is Our Business.* Philadelphia: Westminster, 1949.

Carter, Jimmy, *Palestine Peace Not Apartheid.* New York: Simon & Schuster, 2007.

Cohn, Haim H., *Human Rights in the Bible and Talmud.* Tel Aviv: MOD, 1989.

———. *Human Rights in Jewish Law.* New York: KTAV, 1984.

Crenshaw, James L, and John T. Willis, *Essays in Old Testament Ethics.* New York: KTAV, 1974.

Dahl, Robert A., *After the Revolution? Authority in a Good Society.* New Haven: Yale University Press, 1990.

Doorly, William J., *The Laws of YAHWEH: A Handbook of Biblical Law.* Mahwah, N.J.: Paulist, 2002.

Falk, Ze'ev W., *Law and Religion: The Jewish Experience.* Jerusalem: Mesharim, 1981.

Fernandez, Jay A., "The Fight for Asylum." *ACLU Magazine,* Winter 2020.

Bibliography

Fletcher, Joseph E., *Situation Ethics*. Philadelphia: Westminster, 1966.

Friedman, Paul, ed., *Encyclopedia of American Civil Liberties*. Oxfordshire, UK: Routledge, 2006.

Fromm, Erich, *The Heart of Man: Its Genius for Good and Evil*. New York: Harper Colophon, 1964.

Gaster, Theodor H., "Samaritans." In *Encyclopedia Britannica*. Chicago: University of Chicago Press (1962) 19:918—19.

———. "Samaritans." In *Interpreter's Dictionary of the Bible* 4:180–97.

Green, Joel B. and Jacqueline E. Lapsley, *The Old Testament and Ethics: A Book-by-Book Survey*. Grand Rapids: Baker Academic, 2013.

Gunkel, Herman, *Genesis*. Translated by Mark E Biddle. Mercer University Press, 2020.

———. *The Legends of Genesis: The Biblical Saga and History*. New York: Schocken, 1964.

Gushee, David P. *The Sacredness of Human Life: Why an Ancient Biblical Vision Is Key to the World's Future*. Grand Rapids: Eerdmans, 2013.

———. *Still Christian: Following Jesus out of Evangelicalism*. Louisville: Westminster John Knox, 2017.

Hiers, Richard H., "Ancient Laws, Yet Strangely Modern: Biblical Contract and Tort Jurisprudence", *Detroit Mercy University Law Review* 88 (2011) 473—96.

———. "Biblical Social Welfare Legislation," 17 *Journal of Law & Religion*, (2002) 49—96.

———. *Jesus and Ethics: Four Interpretations*. Philadelphia: Westminster, 1968.

———. *Justice and Compassion in Biblical Law*. New York / London: Continuum / Bloomsbury, 2009.

———. "Reverence for Life in Biblical Law and Tradition," *Journal of Law and Religion* 13 (1996–98) 127—88. Revised version in *Forum on Religion and Ecology* (2001) http://environment.harvard.edu/religion/research/chris_hiers.htm

———. *Trinity Guide to the Bible*. Harrisburg / New York: Trinity Press International / Bloomsbury, 2001.

———. *Women's Rights and the Bible: Implications for Christian Ethics and Social Policy*. Foreword by Lisa Sowle Cahill. Eugene: Wipf and Stock, 2012.

Isenberg, Shaya, "Continue Noah's Legacy by Protecting Endangered Species," *Gainesville Sun* May 27, 2020, F5.

Katsh, Abraham I., *The Biblical Heritage of American Democracy*. New York: KTAV, 1977.

Kennedy, John F., *A Nation of Immigrants* rev'd ed. Introduction by Robert F. Kennedy. New York: Harper & Row, Harper Torchbooks (nd.).

Lewis, C. S., *The Abolition of Man*. New York: Macmillan,1965.

Maston. T. B., *Biblical Ethics*. Macon: Mercer University Press, 1982.

Niebuhr, Reinhold, *The Children of Light and the Children of Darkness*, with new foreword by the author. New York: Scribner's, 1960.

Bibliography

———. *Man's Nature and His Communities, Essays on the Dynamics and Enigmas of Man's Personal and Social Experience*. New York: Scribner's, 1965.

Niebuhr, H. Richard, *Christ and Culture*. New York: Harper & Bro. 1951,

———. *Radical Monotheism and Western Culture*. Introduction by James M. Gustafson. New York: Harper & Row, 1991.

Ortiz, Gabe, "Texas bishops condemn Republican governor for barring refugees and failing to 'welcome the stranger," In https://www.dailykos.com/story//2020/1/14/1911498/.

Patrick, Dale, *Old Testament Law*. Atlanta: John Knox, 1985.

Pilch, John J., and Bruce J. Malina, *Biblical Social Values and their Meaning*. Peabody: Hendrickson, 1983.

Sasson, Jack M., *Ruth: A New Translation with Philological Commentary and Formalist-Folklorist Interpretation*. Baltimore: Johns Hopkins University Press, 1979.

Sorkin, Amy Davidson, "The Leftovers." *New Yorker*, November 9, 2020, 68-71.

Steinberg, Naomi A., *Kinship and Marriage in Genesis: A Household Economics Perspective*. Minneapolis: Fortress, 1993.

Trible, Phyllis, et al, eds. *Feminist Approaches to the Bible*. Washington, DC: Biblical Archeological Society, 1996.

Welch, John W., "Biblical Law in America: Historical Perspectives and Potentials for Reform." In 2002 *Brigham Young University Law Review* (2002) 611.

———. Review article, 27 *Journal of Law and Religion* (2011—12) 499—514.

Westbrook, Raymond, *Property and the Family in Biblical Law*, JSOT Sup 113, Sheffield, UK: Sheffield Academic, 1991.

———. and Bruce Wells, *Everyday Law in Biblical Israel: An Introduction*, Louisville: Westminster John Knox, 2009.

Wright, Christopher J. H., *God's People in God's Land*. Exeter, U.K.: Paternoster, 1990.

———. *Old Testament Ethics for the People of God*. Downer's Grove: InterVarsity, 2004.

Index

Aaron, 10, 13, 15, 51
Abdon, 19
Abram, Abraham, xxiv–xxv, 3–6, 42,
    50, 60, 61, 75
Absalom, 23
acculturation, 34–36, 43, 57
Acts, Book of, 40, 77–78
Adam, 70
affirmative action laws, 65–67
Africans, African-Americans, 43,
    51, 71, 81
agricultural festivals, 66–67, 76
Ahab, 56
Ai, 17
Albright, William F., xxii
Alexander ("the Great"), 32–33
Amendments, U.S. Constitution:
    Fifth, 81–82
    Thirteenth, 81
    Fourteenth, 81–82
    Fifteenth, 81
America(s), 80–84
American experience, 14
American, democracy
    See democracy.
American ideals & values, 83
American laws, jurisprudence, xiii,
    xv, 63, 66
Ammon, -ites, 53, 54, 56, 71
Amorites, 8, 16, 20, 57, 61, 71
Amos, 44, 73, 74
Anarchy, 20

animals, LORD's care for, 65, 70, 71,
    75, 76, 77
ancestors, xxiv–xxv, 47, 80.
    See also genetic connection(s)
    and mixed ancestry.
annual creedal recitation, 59–60
antinomianism, xvi
Antiochus "Epiphanes," 33, 37
Apocrypha See Old Testament.
apostasy, 37–38, 48, 53
    See also idolatry and syncretism.
Arabs, 80
Aram, -ean, 3, 41, 50, 59
archeology, xxii
Areopagite sermon, 71
Asenath, 50, 60
Ashdod, 17, 56
Asherah, 55–56
Ashkelon, 18
Ashtoreth, 54
Asian-Americans, 43
asylum, xiv
    See also cities of refuge.
asylum seekers, xv, 41, 42
Assyria, -ian empire, 26, 27–28, 31,
    41, 54, 75

Baal(s), 55–56
Babbitt, Bruce, 70
Babylon, -ian, 3, 28–31, 54
    exile, see exile.
    Talmud, 31

Index

Bar Cochba, 39
Baruch, Book of, 38
Bathsheba, 36
bats, 38
Beach, Waldo, xvii
Beard, Mary, 47, 81
Beersheba, 7
Bel and the Dragon, 37, 38
Bellah, Robert, xvi
Benjamin, 60
Benjamin, tribe of, 20, 22
    Benjaminite, 60
Bethel, 78
Biblical and American law, xv, 80–83
Biblical period, x, xv, 41
bigotry, 43
black persons, 51, 71, 77
    See also African, African
    American.
Boaz, 49
Blight, David W., 83
Bright, John, xxii
Brin, Gershon, xiv
Brunner, Emil, xvii
Bultmann, Rudolf, xvi,

Cahill, Lisa Sowle, xvii
Canaan, -ites, 4–6, 16–21, 51, 51,
    71, 77
    Land of, xxiii, 5, 7–8, 10–11, 15,
    16–21, 41, 42, 57
Carter, President Jimmy, xiv, 79–80
Catholic(s), 83
Catholic bibles, xiii, 56
cats, 38
cattle, 75
Cave of Machpelah, 5–6
Chaldea, -ans, 3, 50, 60, 61
    See also Babylon.
chariots of iron, 18
Chemosh, 54
Chinese, 43, 83
Christian(s), ix, 43
Christianity, 35

Christian bible scholars, xiv
Christian ethicists, xiv, xvi, xvii, xix
Christian scriptures, xvi
    See also New Testament, Old
    Testament.
Christian theologians, xvii
church(es), x
circumcision, 17
cities of refuge, 42
civil war, xxiii, xxiv, 20, 26
Civil War, American, 83, 85
classical culture, 81
common ancestry, 68, 71
    See also genetic connections.
Coffin, William Sloane, xvii
common or customary law, 49, 64, 81
compassion, x, xi, xiii, xvi, 48
concubines, 24, 54
Constitution of the U.S., 14
    See also Amendments, Due
    Process Clause, & equal
    protection.
"conquest" of Canaan, xxii, 17–21
1 Corinthians, 47, 77
core beliefs and understandings, ix,
    xi, xv, 48, 68, 69, 71–72, 81
covenant renewal ceremony, 59–60
Creation, the LORD's care for, 68,
    69–72, 75–78
Curran, Charles E., xvii, cover
Cushite, 51
Cyrus, 31–32, 58

Daniel, 37, 28
    Additions to, 37
David, xxiii, 22–23, 50, 52, 54
Deborah, 20
Declaration of Independence, 81
democratic beliefs and values, xv,
    79–85
deportation(s), 27, 28
detention centers, xi
Deuteronomy, Book of, 12, 54, 66, 67

Index

Deuteronomic editor, writer, theologian, 19–20, 53–55
diaspora, xv, 27, 28, 30, 35, 30, 39, 40
discrimination, laws against, 67–68, 81–82
divorce, 58
Doorly, William I., xiv
Douglass, Frederick, 82–83
Due Process Clause, 81–82
DNA, 71, 80

Earth, belongs to the LORD, xxi, 74–77
Edom, -ite(s), 39, 53, 60, 71
Egypt, -ian(s), xxi, xxiii, 5, 9–11, 28, 41, 50, 51, 53, 57, 60, 64, 67, 71, 75
Ehud, 21
Ekron, 18
elephants, 37
Elijah, 35
endangered species, 70
Enlightenment, the, 80
Ephesians, 78
Ephraim, 30, 60
Ephron, 5–6
equal protection, xiii, xv, 64–65, 81–83
Esau, 7, 41–42, 60
Esther and Additions to, 37
ethics & social policy, xvi, 15
    See also law, ethics & social policy, social ethics.
Ethiopian, 77
ethnic purity, 59
European settlers, 42–43
Eve, 70
Exile, the, ix, xxiv, 28–29, 30–31, 41
existential meaning of stories, xxii, 70
Exodus, Book of, 12, 51, 67
Ezekiel, 71, 73
Ezra, 37, 59
Ezra, Book of, xxiv, 32, 57–58

Failinger, Marie, cover
famine, 4–5, 7, 9, 42, 75
Farley, Margaret, xvii
fascist movements, 43
fathers of Israel, 3–4, 47, 50, 51
    See also ancestors & forefathers.
Fernandez, Jay A., xiv
Fletcher, Joseph E., xvi
Flood story, 70–71
food for poor and needy, xiii, 65–66
food banks, 75
    Also see agricultural festivals, gleaning, & third year tithe.
food stamps, 66–67
forced labor, 10, 18, 25, 30
Foreign gods, 38, 53–58
foreign nations, 73–78
foreign women, wives, widows, xiv, 18, 37, 53–58, 60–61, 64
freedom, xvi
Fromm, Erich, 85
future hopes & expectations, xxii, xxiv, 74–78

Galatians, 78
Garden of Eden, 44
Gaster, Theodor H., 28, 71
Gath, 17
Gaza, 17, 18
Genesis, Book of, 47, 60, 69, 70–71, 75
genetic connection(s), 45, 48, 50, 59, 60–61, 68, 69–72
    See also ancestors, DNA & mixed ancestry.
genetic purity, 59
genocide, 83
Gentiles, 35, 77
Gentile mission, 77–78
ger, gerim, xiv, xv, 64
Gerar, 5, 7
Gergashites, 16
Germans, 43, 83
Geshurites, 17

Index

Gideon, 20
gleaning, 49–50, 65
Goshen, 9
grain storage & distribution, 9, 75
Greco-Roman world, law, x, 81
Greek empire, xxv, 32–33, 41
    culture, See Hellenistic
    influences.
Guest worker(s), 42
Gunkel, Herman, xxi
Gushee, David P., ix–xi, xvii, 43,
    69, 70
Gustafson, James M., xvii
Gypsies, 43

Hagar, 50,
Ham, the "curse" on, 71
Hanukkah, 34
Haran, 3, 8
Heavenly city, x
Heber, 51, 52
Hebrew(s), 21
Hebrew Bible, x, xi, xiii, xvi, 35, 47
Hebron, 18
Hellenistic period, 32–33
    cultural influences, 34–40
henotheism, 85
Herod "the Great," 39
Hiers, Glen S., 80
hill country, 17
Hispanic(s), 43, 83
history, xxi–xxii, 3–45, 70, 75
Hittites, 4, 8, 10, 16, 20, 41, 52, 53,
    57, 61, 71
Hivites, 8, 10, 20
holy place, 56
holy race, 57, 58
    See also genetic purity.
home, x, 44
Hormah, 18
Hosea, 73, 77
human community, 72, 75, 80, 83
humankind, 69, 70, 72, 78

Ibram, 19
idolatry, 34, 37–38
    See also apostasy, syncretism.
image of God, 69
immigration to America, 43, 80–84
immigration, current issues, ix, xiv
inheritance, xiii, 49–50, 64
inhumanity, 85
intestate succession, xiii, 49–50
Isaac, 4–6, 7, 42, 50, 60
Isaiah, 38, 73, 74–77
Isenberg, Shaya, 70
Ishmael, 50
Ishmaelites, 71
Israel, the name, history of, xv,
    xxi–xxv
    as blessing to other nations, 4,
    75, 82
    Kingdom of, xxiii–xxiv, 22,
    27–28
    tribes & people of, xv, xxi–xxv,
    22–23, 25–26, 71, 73–77
    modern, 44, 79–80
Ittai, 53

Jabesh-Gilead, 22
Jacob, xxii–xxiii, 4, 7–8, 50, 60, 75
Jael, 51, 52
Jair, 19
Japanese, 43
Jason, 35
Jebusites, 8, 10, 16, 20, 57
Jephthah, 20
Jeremiah, 31, 73, 74, 77
Jericho, 16
Jeroboam, 25
Jerusalem, ix, 28, 33, 39, 57
Jesus, ix, x, 43, 50, 77
Jethro, 10, 51
Jews, -ish, xv, xxiv, 43
Jewish people, ix, x, xi, xxv, 32–40,
    56–58, 61, 83
Jezebel, 53–56
Job, 60

Index

Job, Book of, 60
John, Gospel according to, 47
Jonah, story & Book of, 74–75
Jordan River, 15, 16, 17
Joshua, 15–18, 42
Joshua, Book of, 16, 50, 51
Joseph, 8, 9, 50, 60, 75
Josephus, 34, 40
Judah, 50, 60, 61
Judah, Kingdom of, xxiii–xxiv,
    27–28
    Tribe or people of, xxiii, 20–21,
    28, 71, 75
    See also Southern Kingdom.
Judahite(s), xv, xxiii, 22, 26, 74
Judaism, xvi, 35–40
Judas Maccabaeus, 33
judges, xxiii, 15, 19
Judges, Book of, 18–21, 51–52
    period of, 42, 49, 52
Judith, Book of, 37
justice, xvi, 48, 67, 84

Katsh, Abraham I., 81
Kennedy, President John F., 80, 83, 84
King, Martin Luther Jr., xvii
Kingdom of God, 77
1 Kings, 23–26, 54, 56
2 Kings, xxiv, 42
Kindred, kinship, 6, 73
    See also genetic connections

Laban, 8, 60
Law(s), xi, xv–xvi, 14, 36, 57
    See also Torah.
law, ethics & social policy, xix, 79
Lazarus, Emma, 83
Leah, 8, 50, 60, 61
legend(s), xxi, 70
Letter of Jeremiah, 38
Levi, 60
levirate marriage, 49–50, 64
Leviticus, Book of, 12, 64, 55, 67
Levites, 57, 67

Lewis, C. S., 81
"light to the nations," 74, 82
Little, David, xvii
Long, Edward LeRoy, xvii
LORD, the name, xxii
LORD, creator, all that is, is good, 69
LORD's care for:
    all creation, 68, 69–72, 76, 77, 78
    animals, 65, 71, 75, 76, 77
    people, 63–68, 69–72, 73–78
    "lost ten tribes of Israel," 28
love, xvi, 6, 54, 67
Luke, Gospel according to, 50, 77
Luz, 18

Maccabees, -ean(s), xxv
    Period, xxv, 33–39
Maccabees, Books of:
    First, 33, 34, 36–37
    Second, 34, 35–37
    Third, 34, 37
    Fourth, 34–37
Malachi, 58
Manasseh, 51, 60
manna, 13
marriage, 6, 8, 47–48
    with foreigners, 18, 37–38. 48,
    49–51, 53–54
Masada, 39
Matthew, Gospel according to, 50,
    77
Mayflower, the, iii, 80
"melting pot," 33, 85
Micah, 44, 76
Middle East, 43, 78
Midian, -ite(s), 10, 51
migrant(s), xv
Milcom, 54
milk and honey, 10, 44
Miriam, 11, 51
mixed ancestry, 48, 54, 58, 59,
    60–61
mixed progeny, 48, 54, 57, 59, 60–61
Moab, 15, 16, 41, 56

Index

Moabite(s), 49–50, 53, 57, 71
Molech, 54
Mormons (Latter Day Saints), 83
Moses, 10–11, 12–15, 51
mothers of Israel, 34, 47, 50
Muslim(s), 43, 83

Naomi, 63
Nahum, Book of, 73
Native Americans, 42–43, 80, 83
nativist movements, 43, 83
  See also white supremacy
  xenophobia.
Neanderthal, 80
Near East, -ern, 26, 32, 43
Nebuchadnezzar, 18
Nehemiah, ix, xi, 37, 56–58, 59
Nehemiah, Book of, xxiv, 32, 57
Neo-Babylonian empire, xxiv, 28–32
  See also Babylon, -ian.
New Testament, x, xvi, 40, 43, 47,
  48, 50, 71, 75, 77
Niebuhr, H. Richard, 43, 72, 81, 85
Niebuhr, Reinhold, 72, 85
Nineveh, 74–75
Noah, wife & family, 70–71
Northern tribes, Kingdom, xxiii–
  xxiv, 22–23, 27, 42
  See also Israel, Kingdom of.
Numbers, Book of, 12, 51, 64

oaths, 66, 82, 84
obligations, legal, 61, 63, 68
Old Testament, xiii, xiv, xvi, 48, 50
  Apocrypha, xiii, xvi
  See also Hebrew Bible.
  as resource for Christian ethics,
    social ethics, x, xvi, xvii
oppression, 10, 30, 83
orphans, xiii, 65–67
Orthodox bibles, xiii, 36
Ortiz, Gabe, xiv

Palestine, x, 39, 79–80

Palestinians, 80
parable(s), 75, 77
Paris, Peter, xvii
"patriarch(s)," 47–48, 60–61
Patrick, Dale, 63
Paul, ix, xi, 47, 71, 77–78
  peace, x, 75, 76, 77, 78, 79–80
Persian empire, period, xxv, 31–32,
  41, 56, 58
Perez, 50
Perizzites, 5, 8, 16, 18, 20, 50, 57, 71
Perry, Michael, xvii
persecution, 34, 36–37, 43
Pharaoh, 8, 9–11
Phi Beta Kappa Society, 36
Philistines, 4–5, 7–8, 16–21, 22–23,
  41, 52
Philo of Alexandria, 36, 40
philosophy, 36
Phoenician(s), 53, 77
Pledge of Allegiance, 82, 84
Pompey, 39
poor & needy persons, 49–50,
  61–62, 63–68
Pope Francis, xvii
Pope, Liston, xvii
post-modernist(s), xvi
Prayer of Azariah, 37
priests, 35, 57
primordial couples, 70–71
prophets, 19, 48, 55, 72, 73–77
Promised land, x, 11, 16
property, xiii, 5–6, 63, 82
protected class(es), xiv, xv
Protestant bibles, xiii
Proverbs, Book of, 24
Psalm 137, 30
Ptolemy Philopator, 37
Ptolomy, 33
Ptolomaic empire, period, xxv, 33, 41

Rachel, 8, 42, 50, 60, 61
racism, ix, 83
radial obedience, xvi

Index

Rahab, 16, 50, 51
Rauschenbusch, Walter, xvii
reason, 36
Rebekah, 6, 42, 50, 60
Red Sea episode, 11, 17
refugees, x, xi, xiv, 1–45, 63, 67
Rehoboam, xxiii–xxiv, 25
rejectionist attitude, ix
Republican National Convention, 83
resident aliens, x, xi, xiv
responsibilities, 14, 63
    See also obligations.
Reuben, 60
Reuel, 10
Revised Standard Version, xvii
rights, xiv, 63–68, 84
Rogers, Will, 80
Rome, Roman empire, period, x,
    xxv, 39–40, 41
Ruth, 47, 49–50, 63
Ruth, Book of, xiv, 60, 64

Sabbath day of rest, 64, 65
sacrificial offerings, 39
Samaria, 61
Samaritan(s), 28, 71, 77
Samson, 20–21, 52
Samuel, 22–23
1 Samuel, 23
sanctuary cities
    See cities of refuge.
Sarai, -ah, xxiv–xxv, 3–6, 42
Saul, xxiii, 22–23
Seleucid, empire, era, xxv, 33–34, 41
Seleucus, 33
Sennacherib, 28
Septuagint, 35, 47
Shamgar, 21
Sheba, 23
Shriver, Donald W., xvii
Shua, 50
Sidonian(s), 53, 54
Sinai wilderness, 12, 41
    See also wilderness.

Sirach, 24, 38
situation ethics, xvi
slavery, slave(s), 10, 65, 71, 81
social ethics, xvi, xix, 15
    See also law, ethics, & social
    policy.
social justice, xvi, 15
    See also justice.
social narcissism, 43, 85
    See also we group, they group,
    xenophobia
social welfare, 61, 63–68, 81, 53–54
Sodom, -ites, 61, 71
Solomon, xxii, 23–24, 51
Song of Miriam, 11
Song of Moses, 11
Song of Solomon, 24, 51
Southern Kingdom, xxiv, 23
    See also Judah, Kingdom of.
Stassen, Glen H., xvii
strangers, x, xi, xiv, xv, 64, 67
Statue of Liberty, cover, 83
status of women
    See women's rights.
Steinberg, Naomi A., 60
subjective value theory, xvi
syncretism, 37–38, 43
    See also acculturation, apostasy.
Syria, -an(s) 3, 27, 39, 41, 42, 50, 60,
    61, 71, 77
    See also Aram, Aramea,
    Aramean

Talmud
    See Babylonian Talmud.
Tamar, 15
Tanakh, xiii
Temple (Jerusalem), 24, 28, 30, 32,
    33, 34, 39
Ten Commandments, 19, 64–65
Theology of history, 19–20
third Year tithe, 66
1 Timothy, 47
Title VII, 82

Index

Tobit, 74
Tola, 19
Torah, 14, 36, 57
tribalism, 43, 85
  See also henotheism, social
    narcissism, we group, they
    group, xenophobia
Trible, Phyllis, 11
Trimiew Darryl, xvii
Trump, Donald J., ix

United monarchy, kingdom, xxiii–
    xxiv, 23–24, 36
United States of America, ix, xiv, 33,
    43, 65, 66–67, 78, 80–85
UNHCR, 67
Uriah, 52

"vine & fig tree," 44, 76

"walk in the way," 10
Washington, President George, 85
we group, they group, x–xi, 43, 85
  See also henotheism, social
    narcissism, tribalism,
    xenophobia.
wealth, 5, 7, 24, 61
Welch, John W., 81, cover
welfare, xiv, 14, 31, 63–68, 75
  See also social welfare.

Wells, Bruce, 15
Westbrook, Raymond, 8, 15
white supremacy, ix
widows, xiii, 65–69
wilderness, the, xxiii, 12–16, 17,
    41, 42
wills, xiii
wisdom, 36
Wisdom of Solomon, Book of, 24,
    38
women's rights, xiii, 65–66
wrestling arena, 35
Wright, G. Ernest, xxii

xenophobia, ix, 83

Yahweh, xxii
YHWH, xxii
Yoder, John Howard, xvii

Zealot party, 39
Zechariah, 76
Zephath, 18
Zerah, 50
Zion, 30, 76
  See also Jerusalem, Temple.
Zipporah, 10, 15